ÁGI FÜLE
13

BEAUTY EDIT
52-55

Francine Widdows
BUILDING YOUR BUSINESS
61

CONTENT

WELCOME TO THIS ISSUE / 3

lashes — 5

LASH REVOLUTION & LASH BEAUTY 06-07
THE BEST EYELASH SERUMS 08
VC TOOL 09
EYELASH ARTICLE 10-11
HUMIDITY AND HOW IT CAN AFFECT YOUR
EYELASH EXTENSION APPLICATION 14
BRAND FOCUS REVITALASH® 15
READER GALERY 16-19
EVA STUDIO 20-21
PATCH TESTING & UK LEGAL SYSTEM 22-23
CLASSIC VS. VOLUME: THEY BOTH WIN! 24-25
SINFUL LASHES 26-27
ASK THE EXPERT 30-31
EXTRACT FROM BOOK: LASH MASTERS 34-35
HOW WOULD YOU DESCRIBE
A GOOD LASH TECHNICIAN? 37-38
HOW TO EDUCATE YOUR CLIENTS ON VOLUME 39
EXTRACT FROM BOOK: EYE DISEASES AND DISORDERS
FOR EYELASH TECHNICIANS 40-41
NEWBIE VIEW 42-43
NEWS 46

beauty — 49

DO IT YOURSELFNAIL ART STICKERS 50-51
COLLEGE TRAINING VERSUS PRIVATE TRAINING 56-57

business — 58

LASH INC CONTEST 59-60
LASH MEET UPS 62
ASK FOR REFERRALS 63
CPD QUESTIONS 64
INTRODUCING AMBASSADORS & WEBINARS 65
LASH INC ACCREDITATION 66
SUPPLIER LISTING 67-68

I0412256

Passion to Profit Workshop

with Louise Prunty

Louise Prunty MSc Bsc.
info@lashinc.eu / www.louiseprunty.com

Louise has worked as a therapist, beauty trainer, started her own product lines and had distributors in 25 countries. Louise is now an publisher and mentor. She produces Lash Inc Journal and has written and contributed to various No1 best-selling beauty books. Louise mentors companies of all sizes.

A 2 hour introduction or 6 hour intensive workshop on how to turn what you love doing into a profitable business.

Are you sometimes blinded by what you love? Can you see beauty making you a decent income? After all you are doing what you love and that's enough, right?

It doesn't have to be that way. You can be a highly PROFITABLE Beauty Business. In this workshop we will be covering ...

How to get new clients for free. Finding new income streams within your business, how to get free PR, make your brand soar quickly, **Passion to Profit**.

Upcoming dates USA
Los Angeles, Las Vegas, New York.

Virgin Islands
Europe
UK, Ireland, Spain & Poland

Virtual mentoring also available
www.louiseprunty.com
Click on Consultancy

WELCOME TO ISSUE 5 OF LASH INC

Were celebrating our 1 year anniversary!

Thank you for supporting us.

We plan to have many years of great educational content especially for Lash Artists.

In this issue you will find articles and images in our reader gallery for lashers all over the world. We had originally planned to have readers in 4 countries by the end of 2014 but issue 4 was read by professionals in 25 countries. **Exciting times.**

I wish you every success in 2015. Have an amazing year!

Louise Prunty

Contact Name: Louise Prunty
Contact Email: info@lashinc.eu
www.lashinc.eu

Lash Inc.
7 Newton Place, Lower Ground, Glasgow, G3 7PR

Give me your lashes!

Give me your lashes and I will create
Length volume and thickness to make
you feel great.
I'll gently apply to every lash
A little extension, creating a splash!

I'll add length and volume maybe six at a time
Flirty and fluttery, you'll feel in your prime!
They will not feel heavy, they will not feel fake
They'll look simply wonderful,
you'll look so awake!

Give me your lashes, relax and enjoy
This beautiful treatment will fill you with joy.
Maybe some colour to enhance your eyes
How does she do that? They'll say in surprise!

Glitter and sparkle can be added too
Whatever you want I'll create it for you.
Welcome to lashing, a wonderful place
You will go home happy, a huge smile on
your face!

© Kim Gibb

Lashes

LASH REVOLUTION & LASH BEAUTY

AWARDS MOSCOW 2014

I had the pleasure to attend a big event in Moscow in October 2014- the first international Lash beauty awards and conference, where loads of amazing lash artists came from different countries. It was a honour to be one of the judges and speakers at the conference. What I can say? Russians really taking seriously everything about lashing. Some new lash treatments, were introduced one of them, LashSpa- where customers can have a lash treatment, which helps to recover natural lashes, if there is some damage or if your natural lashes are weak.

Myself and the other judges. Lash Artists, such us Petr Lhotsky, Eva Bond, Olga Dobronravova , Tatyana N. and others, had very serious decisions to make : who is the best Lash maker of the year, best Lash Educator, best lash studio, and many more awards.

I introduced my unique 6 Volume techniques which received a lot of interest, and made me happy, also I explained European rules for academy accreditations and EU cosmetic

laws. It`s all about sharing knowledge and Lash news. I have included photos from the event, in these photos you also can see Olga Dobronravova- originator of Russian Volume lashes, oh yes I had the pleasure to meet her

Lash artists, attend as many as you can such events, it gives you more knowledge and you can make friends !
Loreta J.

УМНЫЙ
LASH

Материалы
для наращивания ресниц
№1 в России
BEAUTIER
Выбор TOP-мастеров мира!

LASH REVOLUTION
VIPLASH
BEAUTIER
LASH BEAUTY AWARDS

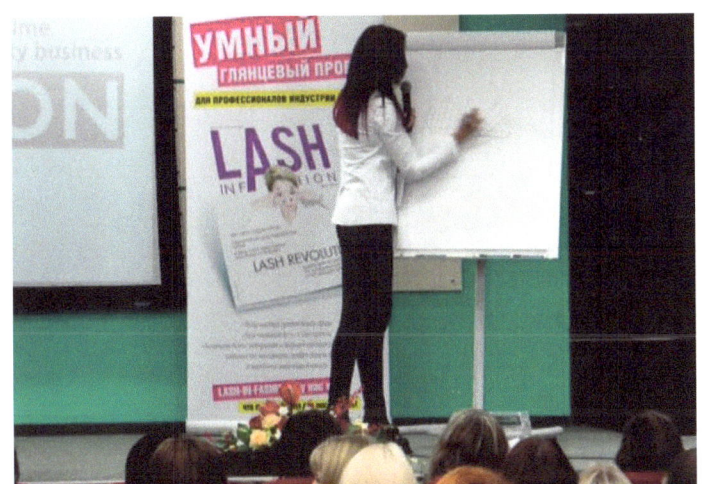

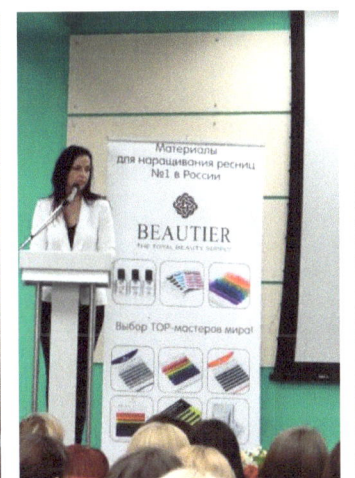

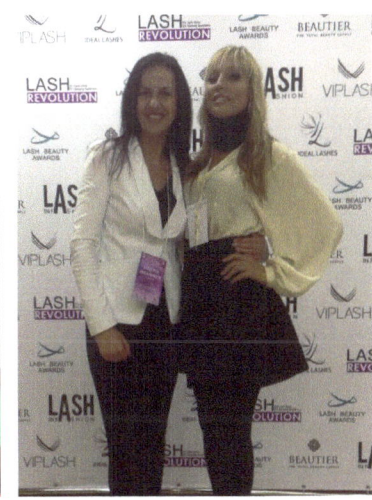

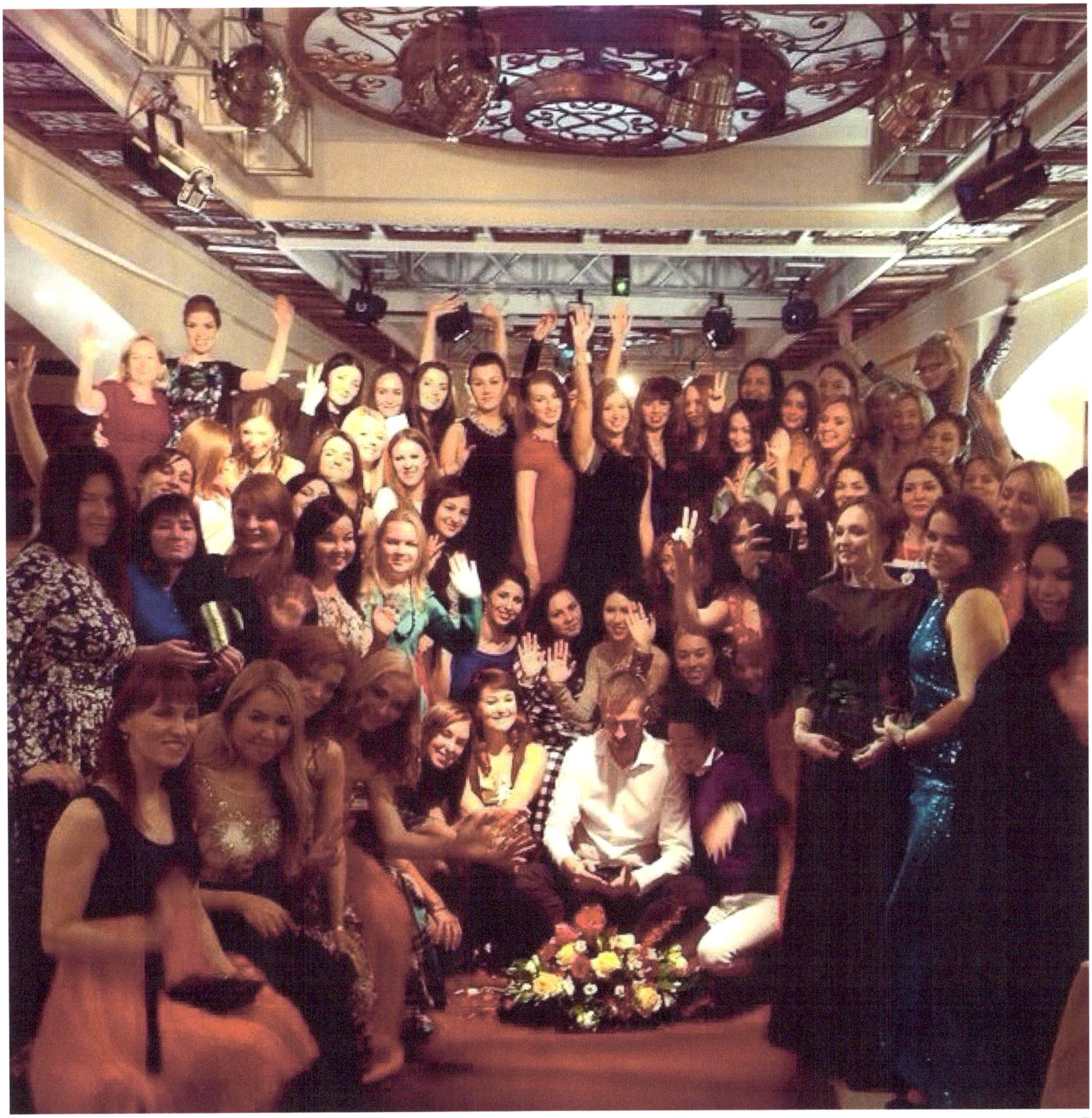

THE BEST EYELASH SERUMS

The best eyelash serums were chosen based on the recent poll on our Lash Inc Facebook group and testing done by our beauty editor. The lash professional favourites emerged. Eyelash serums are a useful product to retail to clients who have lashes that are in poor condition. With regular use they improve the condition and can help them grow back stronger and longer.

REVITALASH

Made with a proprietary blend of functional cosmetic ingredients boosted with powerful peptides and soothing botanicals, the formula lends lushness, curl and luster to each lash.

• Over 97% of testers saw an improved appearance in their eyelashes in only 3 weeks*
• Safe and gentle enough for contact lens wearers
• A portion of all proceeds benefits breast cancer research initiatives
http://www.revitalash.com/

EyEnvy A unique formula is dermatologist and ophthalmologist tested and includes amino acids, vitamins and water binding ingredients, which makes hairs stronger. *http://www.eyenvy.ca/*

FLIRTIES

This amazing product might even convince the most sceptical amongst you! We have tried this with sparse and fine lashes and the results were absolutely amazing!
http://www.flirties.co.uk/lashserum

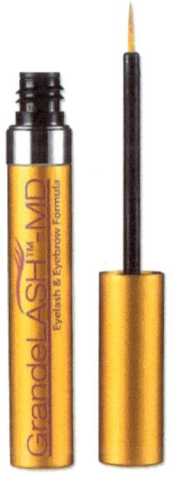

GRANDELASH MD

GrandeLash Eyelash and Eyebrow Enhancing Serum is a unique formula of lash enhancing, conditioning, moisturizing and strengthening ingredients that work.
http://www.grandelashmd.com/

OGENIC LASH SERUM

In tests, OGENIC® Eyelash growth serum is proven to increase the length and thickness of eyelashes. Get longer, beautiful looking lashes in 60 days.
90% of women in a clinical study showed an overall improvement in their eyelashes.
http://www.ogenic.co.uk/

LILASH

LiLash® conditions and fortifies your lash follicles to help create the most beautiful eyelashes you have ever experienced.
http://www.lilash.com/

DREAMWEAVE TLC

With Treatment Lash Construct a nourishing serum that has been clinically proven to work. The peptide, an oil free formulation, thickens the roots and stems, helping to reduce and repair damaged hair follicles caused by false lashes. Can also be used on natural lashes to keep them healthy and strong.
http://www.wrinkleregime.com/

M2 BEAUTE

Here it is, the secret to ravishingly beautiful eyelashes with amazing volume: This highly potent activating serum contains the highly effective MDN* complex. This carefully dosed active ingredient stimulates the roots of the lashes, bringing about a longer growth phase while also creating fuller, stronger lashes.
http://www.m2beaute.com/

VC TOOL

It was a MAN who invented Mascara.
It was a MAN who invented eyelash extensions, and it was another man that introduced it to the western world.
Potions, lotions and beauty enhancements all mainly created by MAN.
Though endorsed by women, with the beauty trade dominated by women.
Food for thought..:)

Hi lovelies, I'm honoured to have this opportunity to talk to you about our new VC LASH toolset.

VC LASH ltd is led by the vision to create innovative solutions, options and products specialising in the art of eyelash extensions in the beauty sector.

We are excited to be able to release the VC LASH toolset that has already had 2 full work shops

Our focus is about making this service more productive.
The main part of the toolset is the wedge; this involved 2 years of testing, extensive prototyping and the latest in 3d CAD technology with a board of investors behind me to finance it and a reputable high profile engineering team in New Zealand.

Like every idea it only proves to validate its worth, this toolset was tested amongst many experienced Lash technicians and hundreds of willing clients all who been an amazing help with much needed feedback, that made this tool successful.

Though it is patent protected, its complex nature of 3 different metals balanced in the wedge in combination with the protective plastic integrated into the device, make it impossible to copy, giving those who have it invested in it peace of mind.
The VC LASH toolset only comes with a 2day workshop for EXPERIENCED lash technicians,
We did work with beginners and found that it took all our time to train them up just for lash placement.
VC LASH ltd like to work in conjunction with other Lash or beauty suppliers of Lashes.
We provide the toolset you provide the accessories needed and host the 2day workshops with many other benefits for your business.

We are also excited to be releasing a number of unique items exclusive to our company:

Posture correction-the new way of using technology using the exclusive set up system that lets you sit up straight, never having to hold your head down or hold your arms up..Why look down when you can look up?....look after your back, neck and less strain on your eyes, no more aching with improper posture or overuse muscle syndrome ....to be released in May 2015

New LASH FORMATION, this requires a tooling system to be made, a completely new way of lash formation, no more adhesive strips, no chance of picking up more than one lash at a time in classic application. Definitely a much easier way to perform volume lash, and no awkward angles to acquire lash extensions. To be released in April 2015

Ergonomic reclining light weight, sturdy chairs made for the comfort of the client and the specifications to work with the beauty technician. These chairs will have changeable fashionable thermal covers, made easy to sterilise and wipe down with additional options for massage and heat properties.
High tec light lamps with an integrated air flow system, LED hydrometer and a foot activated nebulizer in the aid of curing glue at any stage.

Radiant heat covers flip up hover over clients, no more washing linen. And that's not all folks...:)
Our company has many much more to release.
For now we are excited to release the VC LASH toolset, which we are progressing on to get dates and destinations for global workshops.

For now it's one thing at a time..Though VC LASH LTD has investors we are always looking to expand or combined with an existing company and welcome investors who would like to be part of our team in this amazing forward step to improve options in the fine art of lash extensions.
Short of sounding needy, I only ask you to like our FB page just so we don't have to spam all the lash communities with our new and updated postings on workshops or products we likely need your help on, and it's generally the easier way to communicate with like minded lash stylists.

What does VC stand for? Think about the main value proposition you offer clients and why you love doing lash extensions.

Warmest regards
Juanita Shields
Director
VC LASH LTD.

EYELASH ARTICLE
Emma Johnston

In the week before Christmas 2013 we received a call at the salon from a lady, asking for me, the lash technician, she said that she had seen my facebook page and that she really needed some help and advice.

"Yes" I said, I already knew, without looking at my column that I couldn't fit her in.

She continued then to say that she had had her lashes done the previous night by a mobile tech, but on this particular morning she had woken and found that some had fallen out, leaving large gaps in her lashes. She said that she was new to the area and worked as a Nurse and couldn't bring herself to go to work and see patients "like this"

I looked back down at my column, who needs lunch anyway(!), and told her to come in at 1pm, I would fit her in during my lunch break.

She came in on time and straight away I could see that this was going to take longer than 30 minutes. I smile and greet her and take her to my room, I ask her to sit down and to tell me what had happened.

The client explained that her normal lash technician had left the country, so she had looked online for someone mobile to come to her, they charged £50 for a classic set, which she felt was a good price, the pictures displayed on the web site looked good (we later found that this tech had used stock photo's that did not represent her work). While these lashes were being applied the lady said that it hadn't felt right, it hurt and it stung, she'd assumed it was because of the different products being used, no patch/glue test was given, she felt that the lashes were too heavy but they looked full, her eyes were swollen but the tech told her that this swelling would go down, all perfectly normal. She said that when she'd woken up, that there were a lot of lashes on her pillow and that she hadn't done anything that she shouldn't have done.

Ok, I said, lay down and let's have a proper look.

That's when I could clearly see the full extent of the damage that this tech had done to this lady, of course, I've seen my fair share of poorly applied lashes in my time, but these were truly the worst I'd ever seen. I have corrected many types of lashes, incorrectly applied cluster lashes, grown out express lashes and plain old lazily applied classic's, but this really was something different.

I felt sick, I had to tell this lovely lady that she had no lashes to fill! Honesty and professionalism was of the utmost importance here. I took a photo of the lashes and asked her to look, "OK, I said, we do have a real problem here" I pointed out the obvious gap in her lashes which was the width of my little finger, it was also missing her natural lashes, the eyelash extensions that had been used were way to thick, at 0.30mm and were not only attached to each other but also to her eye-lids. Her lids were also swollen from the glue touching her skin, I continued to say that it also looked as though many of her natural lashes were pulled out when the tech had removed the old set.

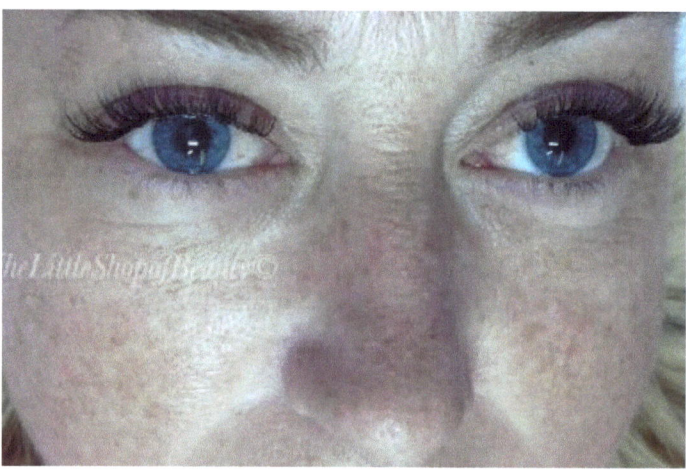

I sat beside her and said that, to me it was obvious that she was someone who took pride in there appearance, so I can't let you leave with these lashes on, they are not a reflection of you and I'm really concerned for your remaining lashes and the health of your eyes. She then asked if she could have another set on straight away? I was honest and said that the gaps were so big that they couldn't be covered up and I was unsure as to the damage that may have been caused underneath.

She agreed to the removal.

To cover myself I documented the removal, firstly to cover me with my liability insurance and secondly to help my client should she want to make a claim against this other tech. I took photo's as I continued to work and again stressed the lack of natural lashes to my client. I was trying to stay calm but was so angry that a woman had done this to another woman, not only this, but damaging our industry in the process. However, to me, it's important to not moan and complain about another tech's work to a client, it's really not professional and perhaps says more about you that you'd want it to, after all, complaining after the fact was not going to help this client. Instead I kept it factual and tried to educate my client as to what was wrong, she understood, lashes out. There were large unsightly gaps in her lash line and the lashes that were left looked terribly weak.

Only time could tell, as I handed her the mirror I told her what I wanted to do to give any eye make-up and some supplements to encourage active growth. I also offered her a course of facials, I did this as, repeatedly throughout the treatment she told me how she enjoyed looking after herself, she felt very vulnerable without her lashes, so why not

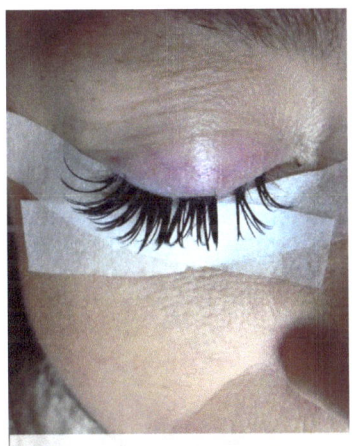 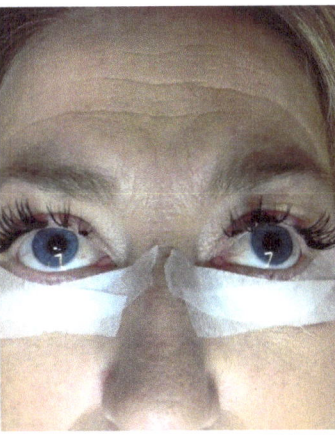 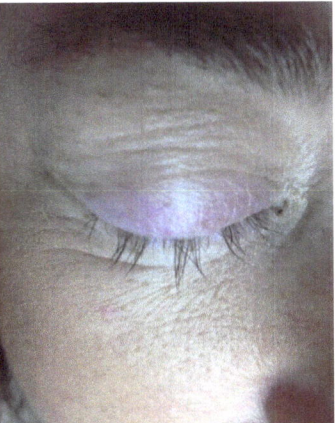 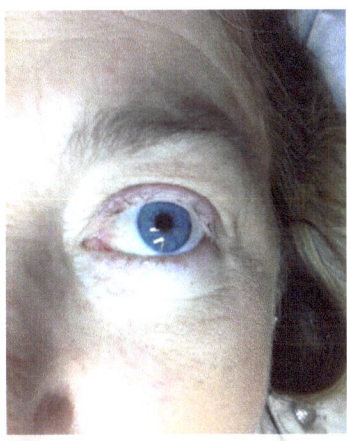

BEFORE

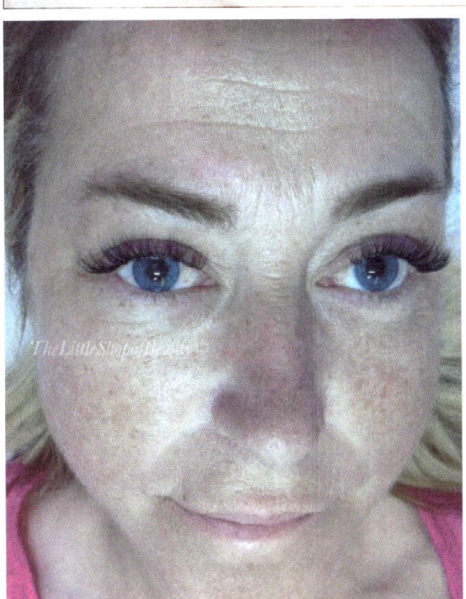 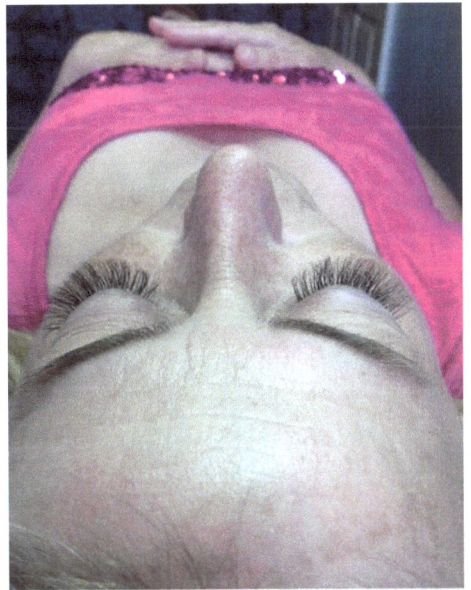

AFTER

the shock was all over her face.

I kept all the lashes that were removed, again, took photo's of these and showed my client that no natural lashes were attached. Her eyes were a sad sight, puffy, red and swollen from where this other tech had pulled her natural her lashes the best opportunity to stay and to encourage a healthy grow back. No strip or cluster lashes for the time being as I didn't want anything blocking the follicles, she could use a mascara, a growth serum, a gentle eye make-up remover that gently melted away

have a pamper and we could also check on the growth of the lashes at each appointment with a view to putting on a new set when they were ready.

She left that day, with a bag full of products, a diary full of appointments, all the evidence she needed if she intended to make a legal case against the other tech and, surprisingly, a smile on her face.

Slowly her lashes began to grow back, each month she'd ask me "Are they ready?" I stood firm, No, I said not yet, I wanted to wait for a few lash cycles to pass.

Eventually six months past and I agreed to put a set on. I chose volume in .05 3D, I was so nervous but also very proud to do them for her and to see her face in the mirror when they had been applied was one of the reasons why I love this job. It was glorious.

Emma Johnston I've been in the beauty industry since 2007 Working in an multi award winning salon until 2009 when I went it alone and founded The Little Shop of Beauty. Started in the lash industry in 2008 in 2013 trained with Loreta Jasilionyte in advanced skills and in 2014 in volume.

Ági Füle

*My name is Ági Füle and I live in Kecskemét, Hungary, together with my daughter, Laura and our dog, Maci. I make breathtakingly beautiful eyelashes for ladies in Budapest, the capital, and in Kecskemét.

*I had been working as a beauty therapist, specialising in nails for many years when I noticed 3D eyelashes on one of my clients. I fell in love with them immediately, and knew for sure that "this is for me, and I want to know all about it".

*I came under the spell in 2008 and this love and passion still last. I keep improving my skills by learning from foreign (American and Russian) Lash Stylists.

*I get much positive energy from my clients when they look into the mirror and admire their look with their fabulous eyelashes. It gives me joy to see that they feel some more confidence with their eyelashes.

*At the beginning of this year I became a founding member of the Academy of Eyelashes where I teach Volume Lash techniques at basic and advanced levels. Our school is not connected to any brand, and we provide our students with knowledge on the highest level, so that they become professional Lash Stylists very quickly. We want to start foreign (European) training courses in the summer of 2014.

*"Aim for professionalism and perfection" is our slogan. Our goal is that the name of our school is connected with training on the highest level, for people in the street and professionals, as well.

*Work done with passion is always fruitful. I consider myself fortunate, because my work is also my hobby, and as I see, I have reached my ambition in business life, too. I urge all of my students to follow my example.

*I have advice for future Lash Stylists and those interested in the job: Work done with your heart, soul and enthusiasm will make you among the best.

*And the inspiration? It always makes me happy to see that a lady is satisfied with her look, and she is definitely glad about it, every day. This is what I call magic.

HUMIDITY AND HOW IT CAN AFFECT YOUR EYELASH EXTENSION APPLICATION.

Christie Vevoda

One of the most common factors that affect how eyelash adhesive works is the relative humidity. Most of us are aware that our humidity can drastically change from one season to the next, but did you realize that the humidity level can change a lot over the course of your lashing day? Depending on where you live, and what your relative humidity range is in a day, your adhesive can respond completely differently for your morning clients as it does for those clients at the end of your working day.

Adhesives made with cyanoacrylates begin to cure, or harden when they come in contact with moisture. This is why it is so important to store them in a moisture free environment. Once the bottle has been opened, the contents have been exposed to the moisture in the air. We each have different methods of clearing the nozzle, and storing the adhesives, but what we have very little control over is the amount of moisture that our little bubble of adhesive comes in contact with as we are applying lashes. That is, unless we are proactive and pay attention to the relative humidity in our lashing areas.

The first thing you need to know is what your humidity level actually is. To know this, you will need to have a Hygrometer. Here in Canada, these can be purchased from the local Rona or Home Depot. I have even found a thermometer/hygrometer combination unit at WalMart. I choose to have a few set out near the different lashing stations in our salon, so I can be sure that each stylist is lashing in the right environment. Don't think that you are exempt from needing to pay attention to the

humidity if you have an air conditioner in the room that you work in. Air conditioning will help to keep some of the unwanted moisture out of the air, but it will not remove enough of it on those super humid days. A hygrometer is the only way you will know exactly what your humidity level is.

One of the first questions you will need to have answered is "What is the ideal humidity level for the adhesive." Each manufacturer will have a slightly different suggestion, based on their particular formulation, but I have found that between 45% and 55% is a pretty common place to start. If your humidity level is higher or lower than this, you may have problems with the way your adhesive performs. If the humidity is too low, the adhesive won't set soon enough, and you will be knocking extensions off of the lashes, or interfering with the bond when you brush past them looking for other lashes to isolate and attach to. If the humidity is too high, then the adhesive will be getting gooey and setting before you even have a chance to get the extension in place on the natural lash. The adhesive will form a bit of a skin on it, and even if you get the extension to stick to the natural lash, it may not be bonded really well. This means clients who call in a

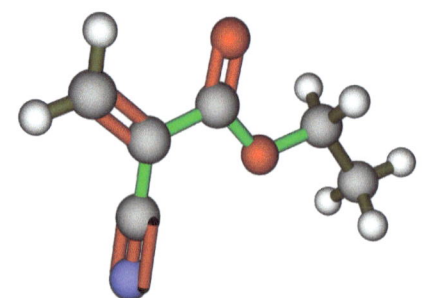

week and tell you that their extensions are prematurely shedding off of their natural lashes.

A dehumidifier will work wonders to bring down your humidity levels when necessary, and even a small humidifier by your client's head will add a fair bit of moisture to a room that needs the humidity level raised.

Understanding humidity and being proactive about the effects of it is one more thing that adds to your skills as a professional, and will make you an invaluable asset to your client and their lashing experience. Remember a great set of lashes doesn't just happen during the time the client spends with you. A great set of lashes happens for the entire time your client wears them and loves the way they look, feel, and last.

By Christie Vevoda

BRAND FOCUS
REVITALASH®

Get the look of legendary lashes with RevitaLash® Advanced.

Best-selling RevitaLash® Advanced is a breakthrough category-leading eyelash conditioner featuring high impact, proprietary technology for dramatic-looking eyelashes.

This finely-calibrated cosmetic formula addresses the visual signs of eyelash aging and stress, by conditioning and protecting them from brittleness and breakage improving flexibility, moisture and shine. Proprietary BioPeptin Complex®, potent anti-oxidants and fortifying amino acids work in concert to help defend eyelashes from daily aggressors and enhance the look of natural, lash beauty.

About the Brand

Built upon the spirit of philanthropy, RevitaLash® Cosmetics is a pioneer and worldwide leader in developing advanced lash, brow and hair enhancement and beautification products. Since debuting in the marketplace with its first product in 2006, RevitaLash® Cosmetics has helped millions worldwide fall in love with their natural eyelashes and eyebrows.

The collection's award-winning products focus on ones greatest assets – eyes that captivate and hair that speaks volumes. Utilizing the high impact proprietary technology of BioPeptin Complex®, powerful peptides and age defying anti-oxidants, creating an environment for natural beauty to flourish.

Founder and CEO, Michael Brinkenhoff, M.D., an ophthalmologist for over 30 years, was inspired by his beautiful wife Gayle to create a groundbreaking cosmetics brand, RevitaLash®.

Gayle became the inspiration for her husband to innovate, create and deliver a collection of trusted cosmetic products that could help meet the aspirations of others seeking to enhance their natural beauty, build their confidence and feel revitalized. In fact, Gayle is credited with naming the brand, RevitaLash, once explaining that the products revitalize the mind, body and spirit.

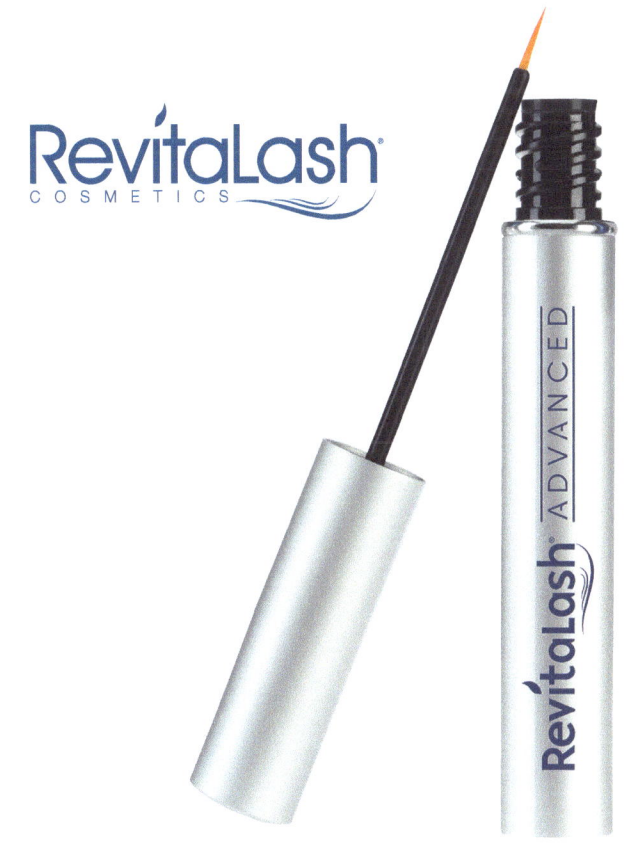

Trust, integrity, beauty and innovation remain at the core of the brand as it continues to expand and lead in the lash, brow and hair beauty enhancement category. The entire collection has gained a loyal following in over 10,000 spas, salons and specialty retail establishments in the US and around the world.

Revitalash was voted as one of the favourite eyelash conditioners of eyelash technicians in our November vote. – Lash Inc

Eva Bond

Reader Gallery

CLARITA SMIT
MAKE-UP, HAIR & LASH EXTENSIONS

Laura Beauty

LL
LUXURY LASHES

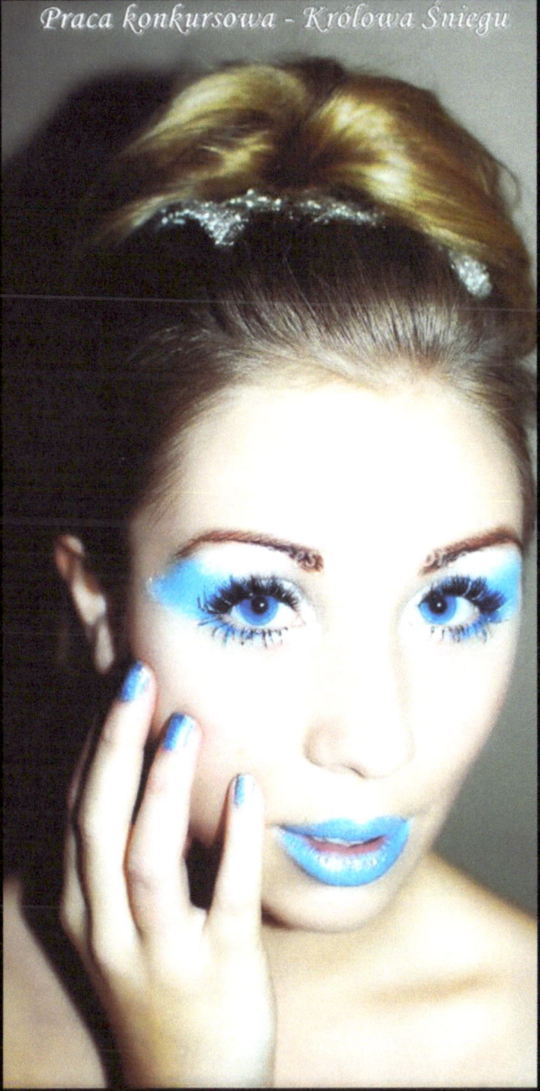

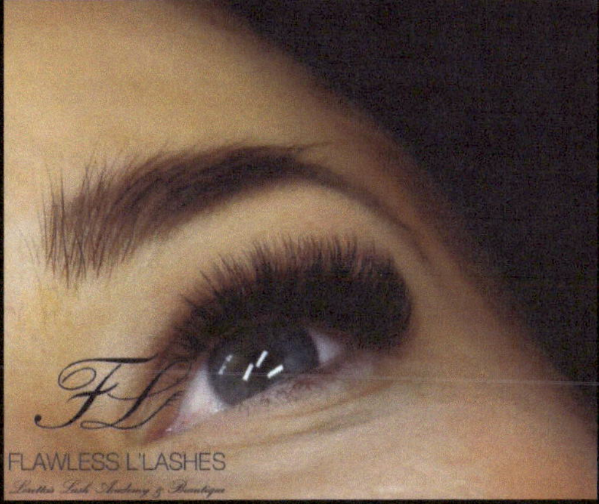

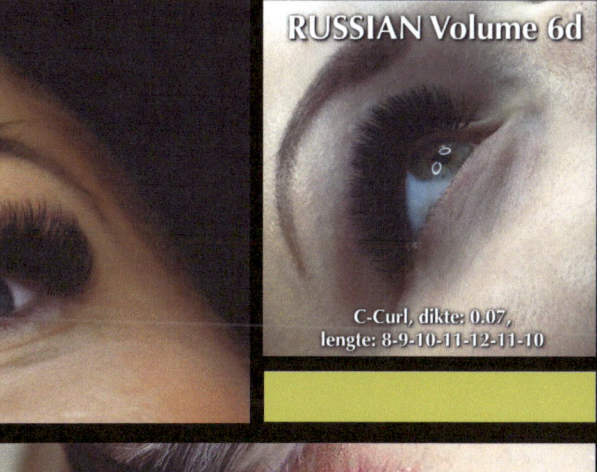

FL
FLAWLESS L'LASHES

CLARITA SMIT
MAKE-UP, HAIR & LASH EXTENSIONS

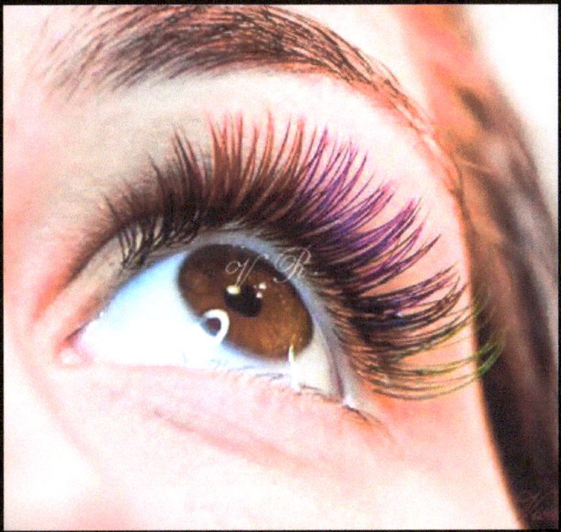

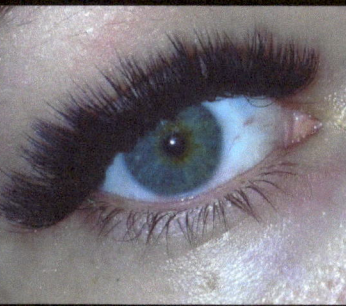

Anett Oranak

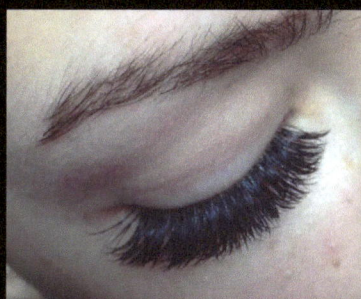

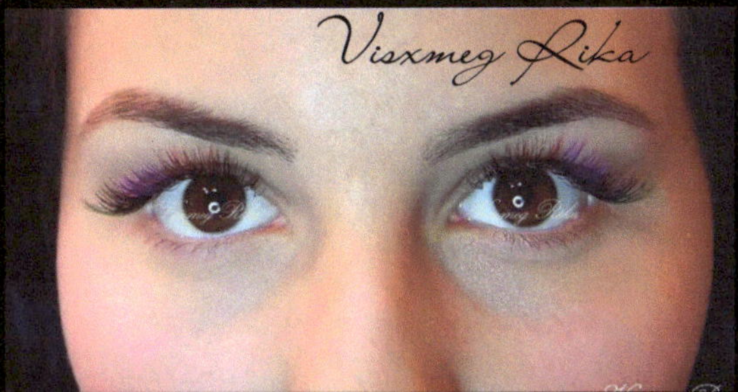

Visxmeg Rika

Jess Martin

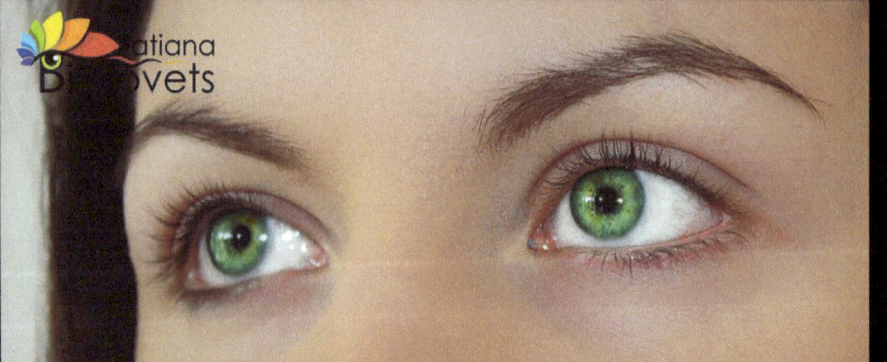

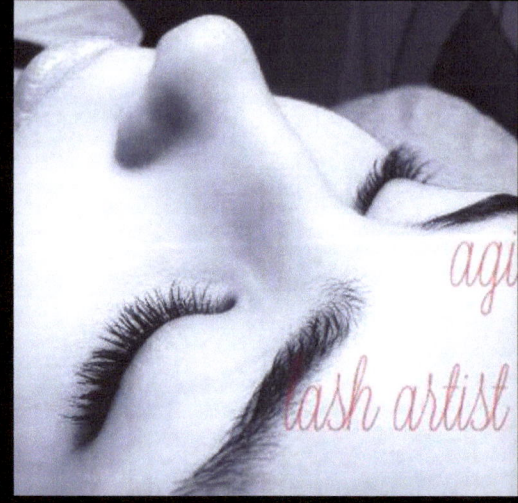

agi
lash artist

Beauty Lashes by Katre

LL
LUXURY LASHES

Jess Martin @ Flutterbye Lashes

3D Volume
www.signaturelashes.com

fule

and trainer

@ lookieloolashes

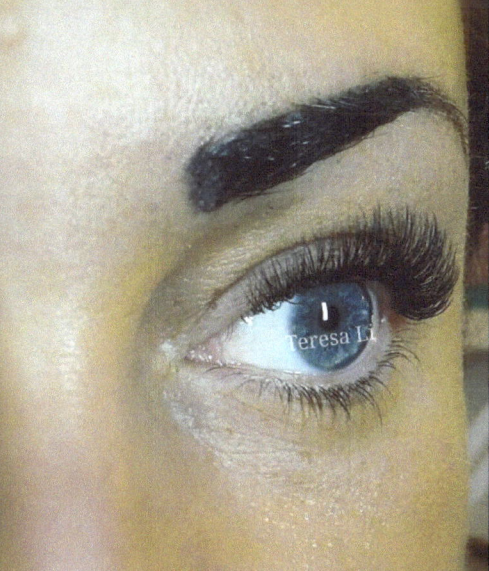

4D Volume lashes by Teresa Li

London Chic

London Chic

Ági Füle

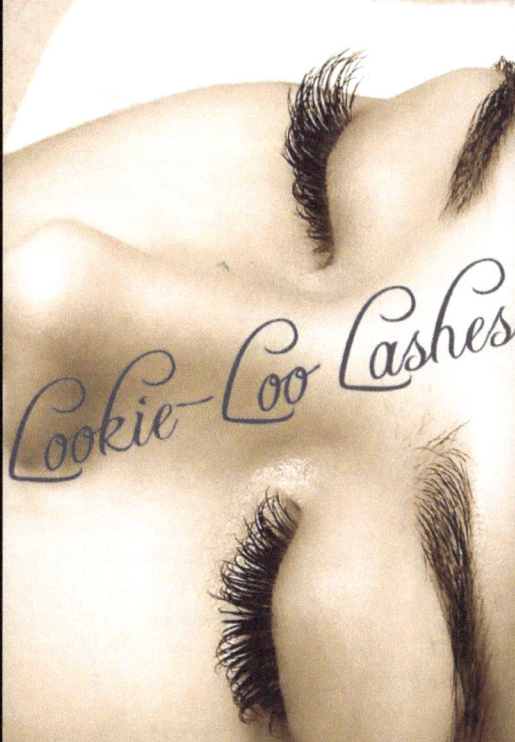

Lookie-Loo Lashes

EVA STUDIO
Eva Bond

THE HEAD OF EVA BOND BEAUTY BUSINESS SCHOOL (MOSCOW), JUDGE OF EYELASH COMPETITIONS, INTERNATIONAL TRAINER, LASH ARTIST.

Eva developed a unique interesting technique - Stereo eyelash extensions.

You will not find it anywhere else. The new technique of eyelash extensions, called stereo, combines eyelash extensions and makeup.

The technique allows you to replace eyeliner and shadows on your eyes by eyelash extensions. The effect is achieved by using different colours of lashes and a combination of flat and steep curls. At the class she tells how to select the best colour combinations of lashes and do it according to the rules of makeup techniques.

Stereo technique involves applying various effects such as Juicy colour, Cleopatra's look, Rock style, Stereo effect, etc. Coloured lashes are perfectly combined with bright elements of clothing and accessories. Such technique will suit those, who are not the adherent of classical black lashes. In spite of the fact, that the technique is new, it has already become popular in Russia.

Hopefully, it will find recognition in Europe and the United States of America and lash stylists will learn the technique soon and will successfully apply it in their work. Painted eyeliners and crumbled shadows are things of the past with the new Stereo eyelash extensions.

PATCH TESTING & UK LEGAL SYSTEM

Dave Hemmingway

My views on patch testing and the current justice system are quite controversial. So please read this article and agree with me if you like, but at the end of it, the current expectations of technicians within the hair and beauty industry are those of patch testing and responsibility to inform, so please carry on as normal for the time being.

As a director of one of the first lash companies in the UK, I have quite a lot of experience dealing with the problems that have been encountered by technicians and I am quite frankly disgusted that the UK legal system and the "where there's blame, there's a claim" solicitors who are allowed to get away with the extortion they carry out.

I am personally lobbying the UK's major insurers to seriously look into the matter of allergies and patch testing and work out who exactly should be responsible for a client's allergies and to face up to the way the beauty industry is being targeted at present. It is wholly inappropriate that a beauty therapist should hold the responsibility for testing and for diagnosing an allergy that a client may have before undertaking a simple procedure like a hair dye or lash tint for example, but that is exactly how it works today. It is completely different to any other industry or the medical profession where the onus lies directly with the consumer.

Imagine walking into your local supermarket and being asked to tape a small sample of cheese and a packet of peanuts to your buttocks and come back in 24 hours before they will allow you to shop. It sounds stupid but is remarkably similar to what we have to endure.

My campaign is to transfer the responsibility for allergy back to the client who is perfectly at liberty to come to your salon for a sample of the product you are intending to use and undertake a patch test if they want to, but ultimately, the responsibility should lie with them and their doctor and not with the therapist who is trained in beauty and not a medical practitioner.

Rant over, and I hope you agree with my principles and will back me when I manage to get the insurers to come up with some positive decisions and we all make a stand together. So, back to the present day and the public has decided that the hair and beauty industry are responsible for their health and well being when they walk through the door of the salon, and who are we to argue with the ambulance chasers as they are commonly known. The world is full of sticky webs and these lawyers are just waiting on the edge for us to fall into one, and when they pounce there is usually a bill for anything over £5,000 to pay; of which your poor client who suffered puffy eyes for a couple of hours will get a grand and the rest goes to the solicitor. Hopefully this will be picked up by your insurers, but if your paperwork is not in order you are on your own.

Should we patch test for lash extensions? The answer to that is no. And I have had a large number of solicitors contacting me for expert advice with regard to this as they were intending to claim against a technician for not patch testing pre procedure. As the adhesive (usually cyanoacrylate based) is a known irritant, it should not be brought into contact with the skin. When we apply the lashes we are always careful not to allow the adhesive to touch the skin at the base of the lash so a reaction to the product is not possible through contact.

Therefore a patch test is inappropriate and could be potentially dangerous. If the treatment is undertaken incorrectly and the adhesive touches the skin then it is highly likely that an irritation will occur and this is often confused with allergic reaction. The only thing that can cause an allergy is the airborne vapours from the adhesive which disappear as soon as the adhesive has hardened, usually a couple of minutes.

Some say that we can do a trial application with which I agree. It will do absolutely no good as an allergy test but it is showing the client and their solicitors that we are being responsible and can also demonstrate whether a client is likely to be irritated by the lashes and start rubbing them. A trial application is usually a couple of lashes applied to the corner of the eye which can easily be removed if the client shows sensitivity to them.

Should we patch test for lash tint? Absolutely! Lash tint and the developer are designed to open up the cuticles of the lash and penetrate within it and also can reach the base of the lash and penetrate the skin through the follicle so will remain after the treatment, similarly LVL treatment products such as the lifting balm and volumising fix also have a portal of entry. Lash tint has a chemical called PPD which is a known allergen found in hair dyes so should be patch tested. Other products used in tinting and lifting procedures do not really need to be patch tested but just to be on the safe side and to fend off any potential claims, Nouveau Lashes recommends that all products used in the treatment which touch the skin should be patch tested.

My other recommendations to lash technicians, other than the obvious religious filling in of the consent and consultation forms in which a client will declare that they have no known allergies and also received and undertaken a patch test where appropriate; is to take before and after photographs of your clients to back up the fact that you undertook the treatment correctly.

There's nothing that stops a solicitor in his tracks quicker; when he is claiming that the client was unhappy with the treatment, than a photo of a smiling face and a perfect set of lashes.

CLASSIC VS. VOLUME:
THEY BOTH WIN!

Leah Lynch

With the industry all a-flutter over the wispy butterfly effects and gorgeously artistic looks created by volume lashes, our classic lash pals have seemingly been overshadowed! Classic lashes are the foundation on which all good lashing skills are built, and getting back to basics to firm up your foundation is essential for any successful lash artist.

Volume is a breakthrough, a true adrenaline-pumping marvel, skyrocketing look into a galaxy only imagined before. We love them, you love them, and clients love them, but hold your horses, artists! There are proper steps to the top and I assure you that taking the elevator from basic classic skills all the way to the top floor is not the way. Take the stairs. It's good for you.

What's in between? Advanced classic lash classes. Some of the top companies out there realize it's more than just classic and volume, that there is a whole world of advanced technique that can segue way a new artist from one technique to another. Think capping, stacking, lash bumps, mink top coats, glitter, and colour. OH MY! Let's entice you with a few descriptions to get your fingers itching for some classic lash fun.

(All of these techniques can be called other things or described differently, so bear with me as I give you my own definitions and terms.)

Capping can be done on classic lash sets to add texture to the profile. This is assuming we are talking about .15 classic sets, max. Picture a client with a hooded lid. You give the client a beautiful L set and then low cap with C curl to soften the profile. Gorgeous! A low cap is done by applying a second lash straight forward, directly below your original lash. You know those times where you apply a D curl on the outer corner and they hook up too much on the ends? Add a low cap of C curl to bring that height more in proportion. A high cap can add height and open the eyes and the capped lash would be applied facing straight forward on top of the original lash. This works in cases where you are looking to add curl to a straighter lash. Capping can also help in a pinch if you have a client show up after a major growth spurt from growth supplements. To cap a gap, simply place one .1 or .07 lash at the base again on grown out but still bonded lashes. Most often, clients will only have about two months of hard-to-handle growth, so after that period you will just fill as usual.

Stacking is beautiful on those with healthy lashes that are set a little farther and fewer between. Unlike capping, stacking is generally done with the lash placed to the side to form a Y shape. You can also mix curl degrees with this technique. One of my favorite ways to stack is with real mink fur lashes. These soft, feathery lashes have varying degrees of curl and add a fluttery effect when stacked on the outer third of the eye. This is a service I added to my menu as an add-on option. We call it the mink top-coat and add 15 extra minutes for $40.

Both stacking and capping are quick and easy because you are applying to already existing extensions. Isolation and placement can be done quickly and fifteen minutes should be enough time at the end of an application to cap or stack strategically throughout.

Another cool add-on service for my classic sets is called a lash bump. This is also a 15-minute service but only costs $30, since we don't use real mink. This is for your clients who seek a liner effect or who are

accentuation (the spot of their longest extensions) is where you want to concentrate.

If we're talking glitter or gemstones, three lashes spaced evenly, cut to progressive lengths, is usually plenty. For color, well, anything goes! Most often, for a bold effect you would colour block by placing several colour lashes side-by-side to really make the accents obvious. For a more subtle eye colour-enhancing highlight, you can stud the coloured lashes throughout the lash line completely. Purple is gorgeous on dark eyes and I have done some amazing sets in tones of brown and auburn for those with ruddy light completions or red hair. Use your creativity to mimic a peacock feather with colour blocks of blue green, purple and gold or have clients add hot pink streaks to their lashes in support of breast cancer and make a donation!

Essentially, what I'm saying here is that there is so much fun to be had here with classic technique and so much to learn and master. Don't

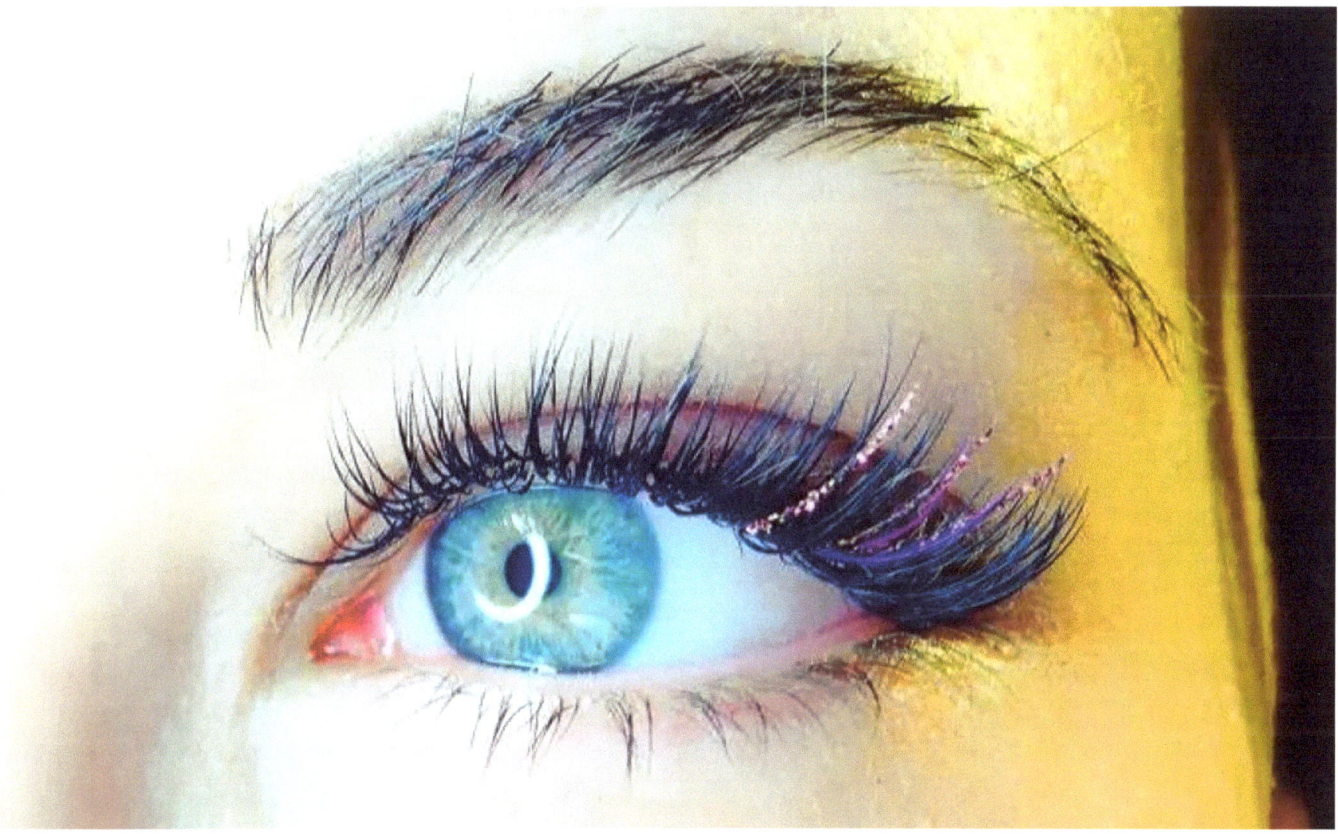

looking for "thicker" lashes. Using a thin sticky gel pad or tape that has been de-tacked a bit, tape back the lashes to expose their under layer of lashes. These fine, short lashes can be extended with short .15 or .18 lashes to add fullness at the base.

Glitter and coloured lashes are my absolute favorite. The artistic creativity is endless and the looks you can create are so subtle but so effective. People hear glitter lashes or even gemstone lashes and think… woah… but, I assure you, they are phenomenal. If you were to break the lash line into four parts, starting on the outer corner, you would generally apply your accent lashes within the second fourth. Applying all the way to the outer corner will look bizarre the same way applying too close to the inner corner would. Directly in their point of

rush perfection; take the right steps to secure a firm foundation of skills before scrambling for that top rung. I recommend an advanced classic lash extension class for any and all serious lash artists. In my class, we cover not only these fun skills, but also thorough consultation, cleansing, different pad placement techniques, taping up, and many other skills that simply must be mastered before moving on to courses like volume.

Happy lashing, all!

For more information on for in-person or online advanced classic lash training, visit larowbeautygroup.com.

SINFUL LASHES

Michelle Meredith-Rath is the owner of Sinful Lashes. Sinful Lashes occupies a 2,000 sq ft Lash Facility that holds 5 lash rooms. It is a one stop shop for lashes and is the first lash wholesale store in Los Angeles for local lash technicians. At the Lash Academy group classes and one to one tutoring sessions are held weekly.

Our Lash Bar is open 7 days a week and services 70-80 clients every week.

The Address is 12266 Ventura boulevard Studio City, California 91604.

SINFUL
LASHES

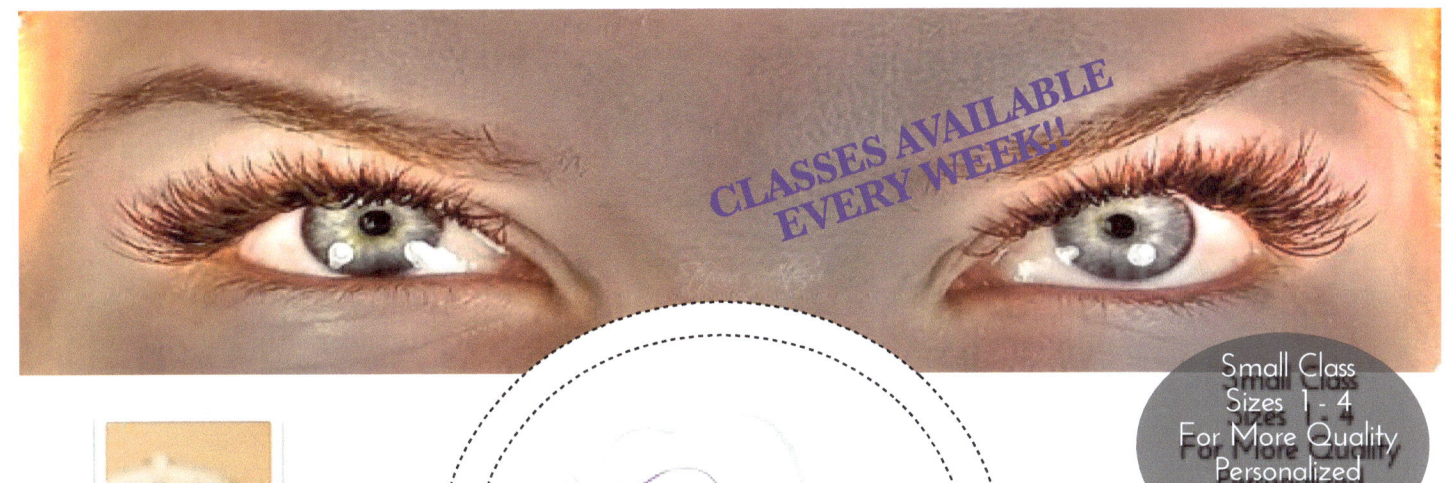

Skyn lash ACADEMY

New Jersey's First & Only Lash School
Stefani Altieri,
Certified Master Lash Educator &
Licensed Medical Esthetician
Co-Author Of Lash Masters Book
Judge & Sponsor Of Lash Wars 2014
Passionate About Lash Education
& Has Traveled Around The World For The Best
Of The Best Training
Certified from 7 Different International Well
known Lash Educators as well as BALAA (Be An
Amazing Lash Artist & Lash Mastery Group
In Beauty Industry 14+yrs Lashing 9+yrs
Always researching for the best of the best
products & 1 step ahead of the latest trends
working hard to bring you the most efficient
way of working giving you all the little details
that most won't tell you to make your job easier.
(tips n' tricks)
Proud Member of NEESA
Certified & Proctor of ADFEE

Early 2015
NEW ONLINE INTENSIVE VOLUME
lash training & mentoring program

lash training programs by Stefani Altieri

Basic Beginner Classic OR Volume Level 1 3/5/7 Day
Volume Technique Level 2 - 2 or 3 Day
Volume Advanced Refresher - 1 Day
Design Artistry - 1 Day
Lashcoat / LashLift / Tinting - 1 Day

Continuing Education at Its Finest
Coming Soon

Train The Lash Trainer - Become A Certified Lash Trainer
Train The Lash Educator - Already Certified Trainers
Online Volume IntensiveTraining & Mentoring Program

www.skynlashacademy.com

all new website   formerly www.skinlashstudio.com
Howell, NJ

ASK THE EXPERT
Courtney Buhler

Courtney is a master lash artist and CEO/Founder of Sugarlash Inc – Luxury Lash Supplies and Adhesives (www.sugarlashpro.com). She is also a wife, and a mother of 2 (almost 3), as well as the owner and founder of an 8-bed luxury eyelash extension lounge in Edmonton. Alberta, Canada.

Other accolades include:
2014 Lash Judge at Lash Wars
2014 Lash artist of the Year – Classic
Top 25 Women in Business – Alberta
Fierce Award 2013 for Women in Business - Essence

Q) I am having some issues with some of my clients having loose skin around the eyes (my older clients). My work looks beautiful when they are laying down, but when they open their eyes their eyelid skin hides the lashes. Help!

A: What you're explaining is called "hooded" eyelids. This look is not limited to only older clientele, but young women as well. We see this eye type on celebrities such as Jennifer Lawrence, and Blake Lively (I myself have hooded lids, also!). When styling your lash extensions on hooded eyes, the aim should be that the lashes rise above the hood to mask it, and make the eyes appear larger and more open. This can be done in two ways: firstly, you can use more length in your set to ensure the tips of the extensions sit higher on the eyelid and the hood doesn't "swallow" them – Or, my personal favorite way of styling hooded eyelids, is to use a specialty curl of eyelash extensions such as an L or an L+. These "L" series lashes are designed for optimal lift of the lashes, opposed to a subtle curl. They ensure a proper framing of the eye and that the extensions sit before the eyelid – somewhat "perking" the area for an instant eyelift!

Q) Do you know why I'm losing the grip on my lash extensions as I get closer to the eye? It's as if there's static or magnetic reaction going on and the lash just flips or twists from the tweezer. It's really frustrating and I'm wasting time.

A: Great question! This phenomenon can be caused by a number of things – give these tips a try and see if you can get to the bottom of it!
1.) your tweezer has static. Metal tweezers can sometimes hold a static charge. Take a piece of paper towel, and pinch it with your tweezers. Then run your tweezers along the paper towel quickly to solve the problem.
2.) Your lashing environment or your client's lashes are too dry. We need moisture in the air for our adhesive to tack up properly and set. If the air is too dry in your lashing area, it can cause your lashes to get unruly. Get a humidifier and aim for 50% RH in your workspace. If your humidity is good, but you're still having issues, use a mister to bring moisture to your client's lashes. They shouldn't be dripping wet, but also shouldn't be bone dry.
3.) Low quality eyelash extensions/adhesive. Lashes supplies are not all made equal. In my testing of our eyelash extension line (www.sugarlashpro.com), we did a ton of research into both lashes and adhesives. Depending on how the lashes were curled (whether they are heated to curl, chemically treated or simply sprayed with hardeners) – this affected how the extension applies to the natural lash. Likewise, the lower grade cyanoacrylates (distilled less times – less pure) tend to "repel" the natural lash, opposed to high-grade adhesives, which seem to "suck" right to the lash.

Q) I am having a retention problem with my pregnant client, could it be hormones causing her lashes to fall off so quickly? Should I even be lashing someone who is pregnant?

A: Lashing pregnant women is an individual decision (both of the lash artist and of the mama-to-be). I know many lash artists who lash pregnant women, and many who don't. What I can tell you with certainty is that hormones absolutely affect retention of eyelash extensions, and women who are pregnant have a whole whack-load of changes going on in her body with hormones! As long as you both understand this, you can choose whether or not you want to lash her throughout her pregnancy.

Q) Confused on priming, do you need to do it? Do you use shampoo type product or more chemical based such as IPA?

A: This is completely up to you, but I'll give you my take on it! There are certain products in our application that cannot be avoided that contain chemicals (adhesive being the main one). With this said, the fewer chemicals we expose our clients to – the less likely they will react. Primer has chemicals in it.
My normal "prep" routine is this:
1.) Wash with an oil-free cleanser to rid the lash area of make-up, and sebum (oil) that we cannot see on the lash line. Some great cleansers are: Chrissanthie, Theralid, and LashCLEANSE (a product we are launching at Sugarlash in the new year). All of these cleansers clean the lash line, as well as prevent/treat blepharitis for optimal eye health. Clients should also be using a cleanser at home for daily use.

2.) Rinse with: distilled water or saline.
Primer (or IPA) still has its place though. For clients who come back with very poor retention of their lashes, I will use primer on as an additional step to the above.

3.) Use a tiny amount of primer on a flocked applicator and swipe along the natural lashes (not touching the skin).

Q) What type of tweezers should I be buying, just starting out and the ones in my kit are not that great, seen X, I , F and S type but don't know what it means?

A: The letter descriptions are all just names of different tweezer shapes that are available from that supplier. Different brands will also have different names. Tweezers are not a "one size fits all" tool. They are very personal, and one lasher's dream tweezers are another's nightmare. My suggestion is to order a bunch of tweezers and see what you prefer! Here are some tips for your first order:

1. If you have large hands, you will need larger tweezers. 140mm is great for large hands, while lashers with small hands should be looking around the 120mm lengths.

2. Determine the "sharpness" you like your tweezer tips to have. Personally, the sharper the better for my taste as it aids in isolating that much faster. I vote for the super-fine tips – however, if super fine freaks you out, opt for the "fine" tips which aren't as extreme.

3. Figure out your curves. Some lash artists use two straight tweezers, others use two curved. Most opt for one straight and one curved/angled. Each tweezer is for a different purpose – one isolates the natural lash, while the other picks up extensions, dips and places. See what system works for you. Play around and see what's comfy!

Q) Thinking of buying 0.05mm lashes for my clients, is there a noticeable difference from 0.06? Can I add more lashes or just the same amount?

A: With my brand I did actually have our lash extensions weighed and tested. As a rule of thumb each time you step down a diameter, you can increase your fan by one lash. Example: 3 x 0.07 lashes, 4 x 0.06 lashes, and 5 x 0.05 lashes all weigh the same. So yes, the 0.05 give you much more "play room" to comfortably vamp up your clients to higher volume stylings! Have fun!
* Keep in mind these measurements are only for Sugarlash products – other brands have different tapers, base sizes etc, and will not weigh the same*

Q) I have read that humidity has an effect on glue, will it cure faster or slower?

A: Humidity is essential to an effective application. Too much humidity causes the lash adhesive to set up too quickly and can cause the adhesive to get "stringy" or gummy during application. Humidity that's too low will cause the adhesive to take longer to "grab" or set up on the natural lash and can cause static issues. The sweet spot for most adhesives is around 50% RH.

Q) Some of my client's lashes seem very smooth and the adhesive is slippery on their lashes. Why is this?

A: Hair (lash) texture can definitely play a role

ASK THE EXPERT COLUMN
COURTNEY BUHLER
www.sugarlashpro.com

in application speed. We all have different porosity within our body hair. The hair type you are referring to is called "smooth" hair. These clients often have hair on their head that can't hold a curl, and is super shiny and beautiful. However, their hair is so smooth and shiny because their hair cuticles are densely packed and rigid (think scales that are laying flat to the hair shaft in perfect rows). This is the most non-porous hair type. Because the cuticles are packed so tightly on the lash, our adhesive can't seep into the pores as well and therefore can slip and slide a bit.

To open the cuticle of the lash: Use a heated eyelash curler and run it over the eyelashes prior to application. Heat will open the cuticle for a better bonding surface!

EXTRACT FROM BOOK
LASH MASTERS
Michelle Ryan (VOL 2 PREVIEW)

I'm sharing my lash story as I really hope it will help anyone who is unsure about taking their lash career further and to hopefully give you the motivation and inspiration you need to take that big jump and become who you want to be. What I am going to tell you is very personal, but I hear so many people saying why they CAN'T follow the career they want and I want to show you why you CAN!

I grew up in quite a rough area and when I was 11yrs old, mum took us to Norfolk for a weekend camping along a beautiful beach and decided we were never going back. we only had what we packed for the weekend and I was livid at leaving all my friends behind at such a difficult age, but in hindsight it was the best thing mum could have done for us.

From quite a young age I had struggled with severe bouts of depression and wanted to "fix" everyone else. After school I decided to make a better future for myself so got stuck into my 'A' levels in psychology, human biology and sociology. I wanted a career where I could help people and psychology, counselling or social work seemed like the perfect choice. A month before my finals I was involved in a serious car accident that put me in a wheelchair, left my right side paralysed for 6 months and my speech impaired. After intensive physiotherapy I was able to walk and had good movement in my arm again, although it will never have full movement or strength. I have metal plates, pins and screws in my body and have suffered with arthritis since I was 22yrs old. I also had quite a nasty brain trauma and after various trips to London Harley Street specialists I was diagnosed with 'severe brain damage' meaning I would never work full time again and my dream career was gone. On top of this I also have a genetic disorder that impairs my liver function. I went on to work part time in a supermarket, got married and had 2 beautiful children. I had the perfect 2:4 nuclear family that I thought I always wanted. When I was pregnant with my second child my

brother came to live with us as he was having his own battles with depression and alcohol addiction. I loved having him around and he was an amazing uncle to my little girl, But I found it very difficult being heavily pregnant and coping with his bad days. We had an argument over something silly and I told him to go live with mum. I was too stubborn to call him and a week later I got the call to say he had died.

From that moment on I realised that life is just too short to be anything but happy and

I turned my life upside down. The difficulties my brother had gone through made me wake up to my own life and appreciate every second of the good and not waste it on the bad.

My marriage ended and life as a single mum with 2 young children (a 5yr old and an 18month baby) was difficult. I wanted to be able to finally say I could do something for myself and as I have always been very independent I wanted to learn a trade that would help me to look after myself and my children, so I went back to college to do a plumbing qualification (Which I loved and I passed my City & Guilds level 2) and I also got my motorbike licence. Finally my confidence was picking up!

I have suffered from trichotillomania since I was small and as a result I always hated my eyes. I really envied girls with lovely lashes and wanted my own! I've always loved doing hair and make up for others, but I have never been one to wear it myself, and I certainly would never have dreamed of a career in the beauty industry! Mascara just aggravated my condition and made my lashes feel heavy and itchy so I would pick at it and pull my own lashes in the process. I had a wedding to attend and couldn't get to grip with strip lashes. Then I saw an advert for individual semi-permanent lashes "Natural looking full lashes that lasted 12 weeks" WOW I was sold!! 45 minutes and £50 later I was left with less than 15 lashes per eye that were painful, clumpy, ridiculously long, plastic feeling and nasty looking. Worst of all they just exaggerated the fact I had no lashes! I was devastated and within days they were gone. I loved the potential for this treatment and I wanted to know more. I have never had confidence in myself but I knew I could do better than that and i wanted to make them amazing for other people!

I signed myself up on a day course run by a really lovely lady who I still respect a huge amount, but unfortunately there is only so much you can learn in a 5 hour course. The products were hideous, 0.25 thick lashes in 15mm. Adhesive which is incredibly slow to dry, thick and poor quality, and 40 lashes was considered a full set. I went on to practice, practice, practice. I spent hours trawling the internet, reading through forums and asking a billion questions. There were no YouTube videos available or Facebook groups so questions were rarely answered and most learning was by trial and error. Luckily for me it came naturally and I picked it up very quickly. Within a very short time I was fully booked.

I'm so excited for newly qualified lash techs, there is so much information available now and watching newbies progress so quickly is really lovely. I had been approached several times about training but I love lashing so much I didn't feel I wanted to move away from that. It was actually my ever supportive 'boyf' Carl who pointed out that when I finished work I would then spend another 3 hours answering questions from other lash techs and that I should get paid for it, so I decided to join forces with the lovely Maureen Blackman (co author of Beauty Masters). I loved it! I had so much to tell them and I was so impressed with the awesome work they were producing so quickly! I'm so passionate about my lashes and I still spend every spare minute between clients reading, researching and learning, posting advice on groups and answering inboxes from other lash techs, its so rewarding and I love it. I get just as excited as clients when its time for them to open their eyes and see what the final product looks like! The huge smile on their faces genuinely makes my day and I have seen such a change in the self confidence of so many ladies, It's just so rewarding. It is hard work but I have finally

found a career I love that never bores me. There's always more to learn and I have a list of several other amazing lash techs who I plan to visit for training next year.

My brain damage has made a huge impact on my life but I have adapted many coping strategies and mostly my clients just find me very scatty and are amused by my 'ways'. My clients are so much more than that, they have become friends and I care about each of them on a personal level too. I see them regularly and share their difficult times as well as all the exciting ones and I feel very honoured to be an ear when they need me and I am happy to share my experiences with them too. I never imagined I would be able to have a career, let alone my own business. My advice to others would be if something makes you unhappy then change it. Those reasons you have for not doing something need to be turned into the reasons why you SHOULD do it. The only person stopping you from being who you want to be, is you. Never stop learning. whether its a new lash technique, meditation, book keeping or photography, there is always something to learn and it will always be beneficial.

Chrissanthie
See the difference
Ophthalmologist tested

Eyelid Cleanser

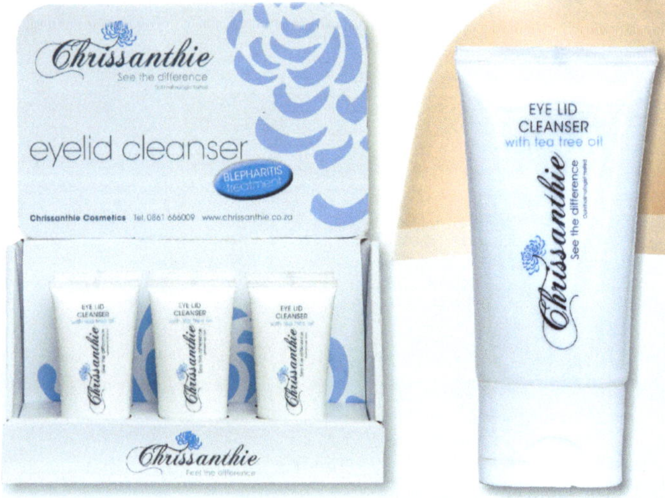

EYE LID CLEANSER
with tea tree oil

Chrissanthie
See the difference

- Completely cleanses and sanitises the eyelids & lashes
- Gently but effectively removes eye make-up.
- Contains Tea Tree and Citrus Extracts
- Effectively treats and prevents Blepharitis
- Will not break the adhesive down in Eyelash Extensions
- Great for cleaning make-up artist brushes & tools

See the difference...

A revolutionary eye shampoo *that is an all in one cleanser and perfect for using with eyelash extensions.*

Anti-Bacterial | Unique formulation | Ophthalmologist tested

*Fast becoming recognised as the **No.1** choice of eyelid cleanser/shampoo for eyelash and eyebrow enhancement wearers worldwide.*

info@thelashcollection.co.za
www.thelashcollection.co.za

info@chrissanthie.co.za
www.chrissanthie.co.za

Now available from:

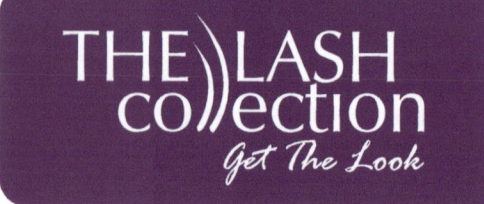

'GOOD FOUNDATIONS MAKE WAY FOR MASTER LASHERS'

Justyna Jakubowska

How would you describe a good lash technician? Artistic..., with a passion for lashes..? Right, but apart from that, they also need to be very patient, precise, neat, and with great attention to details. Unfortunately there are still a lot of under trained or inattentive technicians, who are breaking the rules of health and safety regulations. As a result their work damages a client's natural lashes and in turn gives the whole industry a bad name.

Let's start with training. Most training is very basic and usually takes one day with 3-4 students per class. Following this the student then leaves with a diploma. It is hard to believe that a person who attended such training is able to apply a perfect and clean set of 100 lashes per eye in under two hours (of course there are exceptions).

The problem starts when they believe they are ready to offer their treatments to clients without further practice. Unable to apply many lashes in a short time they try to compensate

WE DON'T DO LASHES LIKE THIS

WE DO THEM LIKE THAT :)

EYELASH EXTENSIONS
by Justyna

3D VOLUME SET OF LASH EXTENSIONS
BEAUTY BAR HODDESDON
WWW.BEAUTY-BAR.CO.UK

BEFORE

the quantity with thickness and length, very often not separating client's natural lashes properly.

Usually inexperienced clients, having lash extensions on for the 1st or 2nd time, can't tell the difference as they have nothing to compare it to. Very often that client will experience pain around the eye area, swollen eyelids, some may even end up in an emergency room with lashes stuck together and a strong belief that this treatment straight from hell is not meant to be carried out on any human being!!! Of course, they'll also let all of their female friends know about it.

The 1st step is to find a good training provider. Individual classes are best as you'll get 100% of your trainer's attention. Make sure your trainer is a great technician too, look up their work and if you like what you see, book your course.

After your training – don't stop! Ask your family and friends to be your models. The more sets you do, the more comfortable you get, more you practice better you'll get and also will notice increase in your speed.

One to one means one lash extension on top of one natural lash. Your clients, apart from looking beautiful need to feel comfortable wearing extensions and any pulling or

discomfort will result in them playing with and picking on that annoying lash, until it is out, usually with 20 others that got in the way. So make sure there's no stickies!

A nicely applied set should last 2-4 weeks depending on how well your client will take care of their extensions. After that time they should come back for in-fills with about 50% of the set still attached. If extensions last longer (e.g. 7 weeks) that probably means, that many natural lashes were bonded together. Natural lashes live between 2-3 months, and when properly separated - fall out making space for a new lash. If more natural lashes are glued together, lashes that are supposed to fall out – cannot, as they are stuck to neighbouring lashes. In the end the whole construction of natural lashes plus extension falls out leaving a gap. If more lashes are clumped together it can result in our client having very sparse and weak lashes.

Some clients ask for super long extensions. Well, it's still your job to advise them on what they can have without causing damage to own lashes.

If the lashes applied will be too long or too heavy you may end up losing a client, as after a few in-fills they may not have any natural lashes left.

With an appropriate length, thickness and separation of lashes there is no need to break from having extensions. Each time when client comes back for in-fills, extension will be attached to a new lash, which either wasn't born yet or in a baby stage when she was here last time.

It is also your job to check on the condition of client's lashes. Their lashes could become weaker if they going through hormonal problems, after certain medications, when stressed or if they don't clean them properly (build up may clog the follicle, making lashes weaker and cause them to fall out prematurely).

There's no excuses for gluing lashes together- if you can't see the little lashes, get magnifying glasses or get better light, and those technicians who apply extensions in client's home on the floor with no proper light, well- do it right or don't do it at all!

Education and training never ends, further your lash skills with more advanced lash training courses. Invest in yourself, you're worth it!

Be fabulous lash artists and spread the lash love.

HOW TO EDUCATE YOUR CLIENTS ON VOLUME
Olga Villarreal

A lot of us have gone through Volume Eyelash training, maybe even more than once. Have struggled through it. Have practiced, practiced and done some more practice to get it right. Our models have loved it. We feel good and now we want to start offering the service to all our clients new and old.

Now the questions start coming up. How is it going to look? Does it really last longer? Does it look as good as classic?

Is it really full? Can they be long too?

Lets not forget about the price increase, This might be one of the highest factors that is considered.

How are they going to budget for it or account for it?

Volume eyelash extensions are not the same as classic lashes in many ways. You can create as full and beautiful look as some clients demand but with a more natural look.

Clients can be very skeptical at first if they had classic lashes for a while. The best way to introduce volume is doing a hybrid where you mix in classic with volume. This way they keep some of the bold look the classic lashes give and it gives a good intro to getting used to the volume lashes.

The way I explain to my clients is letting them feel the lashes and showing the different looks.

How soft and more natural looking they are.

When you do your consultation for their first set explain all the key points of how much longer they last and what the real price difference is. Instead of coming in every two weeks they would be seeing you every three weeks and maybe be able to go even longer between fills.

Educate your client on how volume eyelash extensions gives the opportunity for someone with sparse or super fine lashes to have a full set of lashes. For those clients who always want MORE. The ultra light weight in Volume lashes gives us the ability to apply multiple lashes per single natural lash without damaging the natural lashes. Something that would be a good key point on those clients you want to start introducing volume to.

Take a note of the clients that like that very natural look and explain to them, volume doesn't necessary means crazy fullness. There is a very natural settled volume look in volume that can be achieved. The best thing about that nice settled look is, when they fall out it's a very natural look, while with it classic can sometimes look like you have gaps.

"Can they still be long?" was one of many questions my clients had at the beginning.

At first I didn't know how to answer this. Since mainly I thought about how great it is to add volume on clients lashes. Yes they CAN be as long as classic lashes and full at the same time. The idea is to follow the main rules you use when applying classic lashes. You don't want to go too long or give too much weight to the natural lash. Once they see how beautiful and full they look, the length won't matter as much.

CONDITIONS YOU MAY COME ACROSS IN A CONSULTATION WITH YOUR CLIENT.

Cataract is a condition which leads to a clouding of the eye lens. This causes blurred vision and is one of the most common causes of blindness. Cataract occurs when light is obstructed from passing the lens and reaching the retina. The most common cause of cataract is ageing; however, it can also occur as a result of trauma, radiation, genetics and drug use. People who suffer from cataract often have trouble driving, reading and recognizing others.

SYMPTOMS

Cataract affects the eyes in many ways. Some sufferers don't experience blurred vision, but find it difficult to recognise certain colours, changes in contrast and glare from bright lights. Symptoms that could occur after surgery include retinal detachment and endophthalmitis. In these cases, patients will often experience pain and will become more sensitive to bright lights.

TREATMENT

Surgery is the only form of treatment and can be performed at any age. Surgery is always conducted under local anaesthesia and roughly 90% of patients regain full vision. Phacoemulsification is the most common form of surgery used for cataract treatment. After an operation patients must not strain their eyes or undertake heavy lifting for around one month. There is currently no known prevention method for cataract apart from weak evidence to suggest that vitamin A, B and C could help.

CORNEAL DISEASE

Corneal disease directly affects the cornea – the clear tissue in the front of the eye which

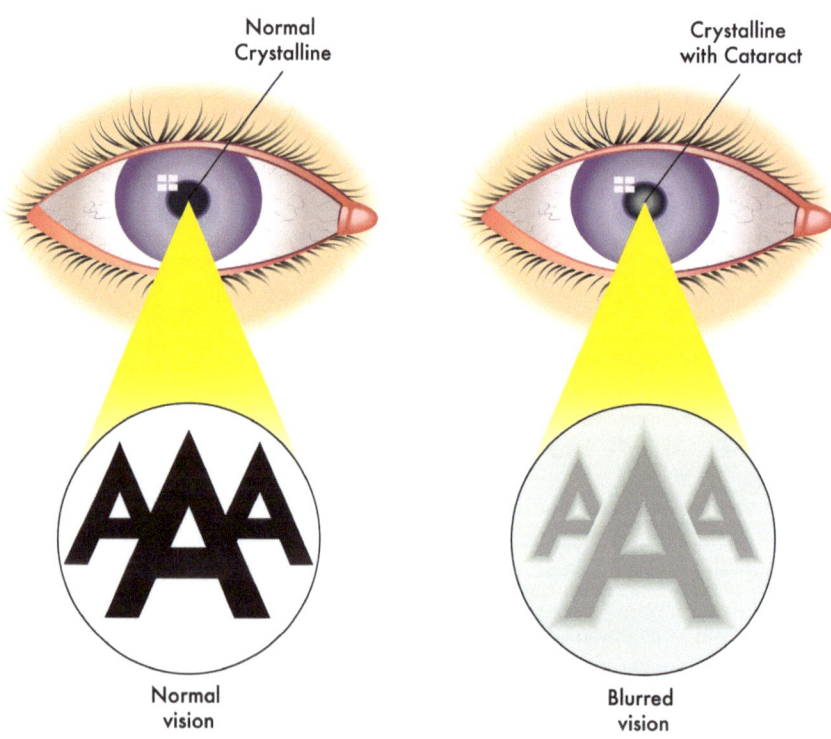

CATARACT

Normal Crystalline

Crystalline with Cataract

Normal vision

Blurred vision

allows light to pass through to the retina. Corneal disease either affects the clarity or curvature of the cornea, which results in blurred vision. It can be caused through infections, trauma, autoimmune disorders, genetics and inflammatory diseases.

SYMPTOMS

Corneal disease can cause severe pain if the cornea is torn as it can affect nearby nerves. The most common symptoms include sensitivity to light, irritation and blurred vision.

TREATMENT

Treatment for corneal disease will vary depending on the underlying condition. In some circumstances surgery may be required, while in others laser eye treatment or prescription antibiotics may suffice. Good general hygiene and regular vaccinations are the best preventative measures. Sunglasses with 100% ultraviolet block will also minimize damage from the sun's rays, and diets heavy in omega-3 fatty acids are also recommended.

DIABETIC RETINOPATHY

Diabetic retinopathy is a common condition associated with diabetes, and if it's left untreated it can result in blindness. Diabetic retinopathy is caused by high blood sugar levels which damage the cells in the eye. The retina requires a constant supply of blood, which is fed through small blood vessels. High blood sugar can cause these vessels to block or leak, which stops the retina from working. Scientists state that 90% of diabetic retinopathy cases could be reduced if patients had more frequent eye checks. The longer people suffer from diabetes, the higher the chance they'll have of suffering from diabetic retinopathy. Almost all patients that have been suffering from type I diabetes for over 20 years have some degree of the condition.

SYMPTOMS

Anyone who suffers from diabetes should have their eyes regularly examined; symptoms may not occur until it's too late, so it's important that it's identified and treated as soon as possible. Late stage symptoms could include floaters, blurred vision and sudden blindness.

TREATMENT

Treatment of diabetic retinopathy will vary depending on the stage it has reached. If caught early it can be treated through correct diabetes management. When it has reached advanced stages, laser eye surgery can be used to prevent further damage. The best preventative measure is to have regular screenings and keep blood sugar levels as normal as possible.

DRY EYE SYNDROME

Dry eye syndrome, also known as dry eye disease, occurs when either the eyes don't make enough tears or the tears evaporate too quickly. The condition leads to inflamed and irritated eyes. If it is caused by a blockage of the oil glands, it's called blepharitis. There are a number of different causes, such as hot and windy climates, hormonal changes,

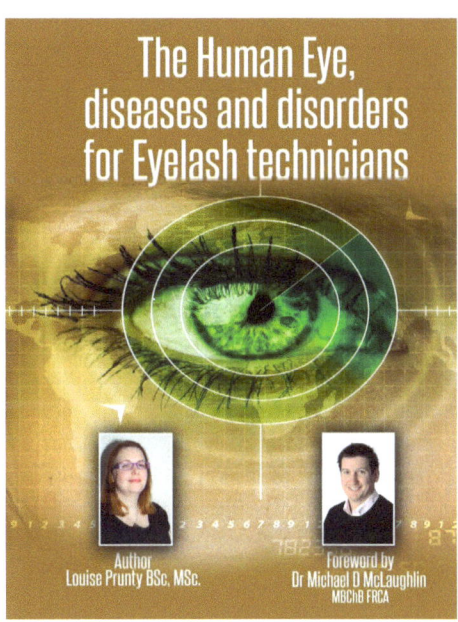

The Human Eye, diseases and disorders for Eyelash technicians

Author
Louise Prunty BSc, MSc.

Foreword by
Dr Michael D McLaughlin
MBChB FRCA

medication side effects and aging. It's rarely a serious condition, unless it has been caused by an inflammation or problem associated with another disease.

SYMPTOMS

Dry and sore eyes are the most common symptoms. Blurred vision, heavy watering, grittiness and burning can also occur. Symptoms will often get worse in warmer conditions and prolonged dry eye syndrome can significantly increase the chance of other eye disorders from occurring. Severe symptoms may also be a side effect of cornea scarring.

TREATMENT

Dry eye syndrome must be treated straight away; otherwise it could cause permanent eye damage. Eye drops are the most common form of treatment as they will provide the lost lubrication. Surgery may be required to block drainage tear ducts which cause leakages. There are various forms of prevention and after-treatment, including using a humidifier to moisten the air, not sitting in front of a fire, avoiding eye strain from computers or television screens, and having a diet high in omega-3 fatty acids.

GLAUCOMA

Glaucoma is a category of conditions which affects vision, often in both eyes on varying levels. It is caused by blockages in the drainage ducts, which prevents fluid from flushing efficiently. The pressure caused by this excess fluid can damage the optic nerve and retina. There are four primary types of glaucoma:

Chronic open-angle glaucoma – this usually develops slowly with age and is the most common form.

Primary angle-closure glaucoma – this often causes sudden pains and can develop either slowly or suddenly.

Secondary glaucoma – this is often caused by other eye conditions and inflammations.

Developmental glaucoma – this usually develops soon after birth and can be very serious.

SYMPTOMS

Most cases of glaucoma don't present any symptoms as it usually develops slowly. The first part of the eye to be affected is the peripheral vision, after which, it slowly works its way to the centre. Other symptoms could include intense pain, headaches, tenderness, misty vision, light sensitivity and loss of vision. Typical progression to blindness usually takes between 25 to 70 years without any treatment.

TREATMENT

Treatment revolves around reducing pressure in the eye. This could include switching to glasses instead of using contact lenses, using prescription eye drops, laser treatment and surgery to remove the blockage. Pressure can also be treated with eye drops. While these treatments can provide a temporary solution, none of them will solve the problem permanently as there is currently no cure.

*Available from
https://www.createspace.com/4913125
Or bookstores.*

NEWBIE VIEW
Martha J. Bianco

We all know that most clients have no idea of what it takes to be a good lash artist. I can't say that I blame them, considering the depth of my own ignorance just two short years ago, in 2012. Incredibly, this was my plan: I'd take the training on Dec. 2 and issue my first Groupon by Dec. 15 – in time for the Christmas rush. That's right: A Groupon.

The first pop in my bubble was the awareness that I would not be able to provide clients with a full set of eyelashes by Easter, let alone Christmas. I think my top speed back then was 35 lashes per eye in 6 hours. Then there was the fact that to Groupon, I was a nothing, a nobody, a newbie in an already overcrowded beauty market.

I could have given up, but being clearly of the obsessive-compulsive persuasion, I persevered. I focused on developing a web presence and on improving my speed by giving away lashes to whoever would show up. After several months, I started advertising on Facebook (I had created a pretty decent website, Yelp page, and FB page by that point), letting people know that I would do practice lash extensions for $25. I charged a little less than the going rate for those who hung on for fills. I slowly began to acquire a few clients and some positive reviews and FB likes. These were what Groupon wanted in order to allow me to launch a promotion with them.

In November of 2013, nearly a full year after my training, I finally ran my first Groupon. My Groupon price was low, and I found that those clients who could afford the Groupon couldn't afford the fills. Still, I continued to get some loyal clients and book return fills. By this time, I could complete a new full set of about 100 lashes per eye in about 2.5 hours. In February 2014, just over a year after being licensed in classic lashes, I took a volume lash extension course, figuring that that was what I needed to separate me from everyone else. I advertised myself as being among the first volume lasher in Oregon, and I raised my Groupon and my fill prices.

Now, here I am, nearly two year since first becoming certified in classic lashes and 8 months into volume. I have once again raised my Groupon price to target clients who can afford to come back for fills. It takes me 3.5 hours to do a full volume set (350-400 lashes per eye). I no longer do classics. I have begun to interact professionally with colleagues around the world, waking up each day wondering what new trick, tip, or technique I will learn, looking forward to taping and lashing and sharing, continuing to learn and grow in this fascinating field that I love so dearly. Two years ago I had no idea what I was in for, and today I look forward to the future with much anticipation, wondering where I will be two years from now! One thing is for sure: I need to reign in my expectations. For now my goal is finish a beautiful set of two-hour lashes. I'll set aside any more unrealistic goals (competitions, anyone?). For now.

Martha J. Bianco

Lash Crush at La Bellissima

Before & After
Eyelash Extensions

First Set of Extensions Completed,
12/2/2012

By Martha Bianco
Lavish Lashes-Cert8ified Artist
&
Owner, La Bellissima Salon

Same Model, Extensions Completed
One Year After Certification
12/2/2013

WWW.LA-BELLISSIMA.COM

Same Model with Volume Lashes
November 2014

COSMOPROF ASIA

The exhibition, which was held on 12-14 November at the Hong Kong Convention and Exhibition Centre, attracted close to 60,000 visitors from all over the world and almost 64% of them came from 93 non-Asian countries. The international attendance confirmed Cosmoprof Asia as the leading beauty B2B event in the Asia Pacific region.

New exhibiting areas and initiatives increased the business opportunities for professionals from all over the world, and the comprehensive educational programme at this year's show, including 13 different presentations over the three show days, covered the widest scope of topics yet including spa and wellness, nail, eyelash, make up, beauty trends, market updates as well as innovation and formulation.

The next edition of Cosmoprof Asia will take place in Hong Kong on 11 -13 November, 2015. For more information
www.cosmoprof-asia.com

NOVALASH LAUNCHES LUXURIOUS LINE OF FAUX MINK LASH EXTENSIONS

NovaLash launched its own line of luxurious faux mink lash extensions called novaMINX mix. Intended to mimic the properties of real mink fur, novaMINX mix are extremely light weight, soft and supple with a high gloss finish.

Each box is designed to contain the correct proportion of varying lengths for precise application of NovaLash's three-length bonding technique, which works with the three phases of the natural lash growth cycle. novaMINX mix are priced at £24 per box and available for purchase through NovaLash.

Twitter: @novalashlondon
Facebook: www.facebook.com/novalashus

LASHES FOR LIFE

Lashes for Life is a non-profit organisation set up by Jenelle Paris from Lash Affair. Lashes for Life funds eyelash extension treatments for women affected by cancer. A percentage of all Lash Affair proceeds goes directly to Lashes for Life so that our community of Lash Artists is able to beautifully impact women on a large scale.
http://lashesforlife.com/

THE LIFE & TIMES OF LILLY THE LASH BY JULIE WOIK

For any lash lovers with children we recommend the first in this series of books. The Life and Times of Lilly the Lash is a series of fascinating children's books, in which an eyelash teaches life lessons and the importance of self-esteem. Adventurous, yet meaningful storylines told in rhythm and rhyme, accompanied by colourful illustrations, provide the main character with a marvellous opportunity to teach children valuable lessons. Available from Amazon and various larger bookstores.

LASH MASTERS VOL 2 DUE FOR RELEASE EARLY 2015.

Lash Masters Vol 1 was an international best seller. It is anticipated that Vol 2 will sell just as many bringing valuable business insights and inspiration to the world of lash technicians.

Co-authors included in the book are...
Petr Lhotský
Linh Nguyen
Michelle Ryan
Laura Besenyei
Luisa Krayem
Vivian Ko
Lesya Zakharova
Olga Volkova

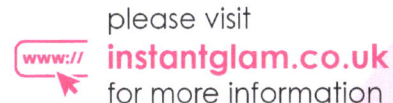

please visit
instantglam.co.uk
for more information

VOLUME LASH TRAINING COURSE FROM INSTANT GLAM

WIN

✓ To be in with a chance of winning email **sarah@lashinc.eu** with the subject line: **Competition**
Closing date: 14th March 2015

✓ An email will be chosen at random to win the training prize.
Competition sponsored by Instant Glam.

🌐 www.instantglam.co.uk   ✉ info@instantglam.co.uk

INFORMATION PRODUCTS TO DEVELOP YOURSELF AND YOUR BUSINESS

This professional eyelash extensions guide is a aimed at students that have a good understanding of the application of single extensions and would now like to enhance their skills and perfect their techniques. This guide includes detailed illustrations covering a number of advanced techniques that will improve the standard and quality of your work. Learn how to access eye and face shapes and to create the perfect lash styles. Understand how to mix curls within your sets to create unique looks. Improve your lash set up, application speed, Isolation and uniformity of lashes in your sets and much, much more. The essential guide for the serious lash tech.

£39.99 from www.lashinc.eu shop or www.amazon.co.uk

FOUNDATION TECHNIQUES DVD

'Whether you are new to the industry, newly qualified or just looking to refresh your skills, this DVD is a must for all serious lash technicians.
In this DVD I fully explain and demonstrate a complete application in an easy to follow step by step guide.
Packed with hints, tips and proper guidance this DVD provides all the necessary and essential information to create beautiful lashes from start to finish.'

DVD £39.95 from www.lashinc.eu shop or www.amazon.co.uk or buy DVD & Book for £69 from www.lashinc.eu

THE HISTORY OF EYELASH EXTENSIONS

The history of eyelash extensions cover strip lashes, cluster, semi permanent eyelash extensions and volume. The development of extending eyelashes throughout the ages.

£15.99 from www.lashinc.eu or www.amazon.com

Beauty

DO IT YOURSELF NAIL ART STICKERS

Ruth Morrison

January can be a quieter month for salon's when clients are recovering from the festive period. Along with January offers to tempt clients to come to the salon, you can use any free time you may have to prepare for the busy times that will return.

This idea can be used to promote nail services, and could also be offered as a free add on to entice clients through the door. The great thing about this is that it can be done in advance, you can have them all ready, just waiting to be added onto nail services saving time, but adding that little bit extra for your client to admire. It can be promoted as a bespoke and personalised touch for your clients, and should any of your clients request something particular, you can use this method to have their personalised nail art ready in advance, and really give the wow factor without your clients having to sit in the manicure chair for long periods while you hand paint.

The two examples I have prepared are extremely simple but as you can see, can change a simple French or coloured gel polish into something more arty and interesting.

Arabella nail forms are great to prepare all your nail art stickers, although a non-stick smooth surface can be used, the shiny side of used nail forms and poly pockets can be used as well, you could even pop photo's, pictures or guide drawings into the poly pocket beforehand to use as a guide to work to.

If you are going to be using light colours it is a good idea to lay a white background down first, this will help the colours to pop when applied onto the nail, especially if it is applied on top of a dark background.

The roses are very, very simple to do, using your desired brand of gel polish or coloured

gel use a dotting tool, or a toothpick, and lay down your chosen choice of colours. You can experiment with more colours and the ratio of colours to get different effects. Keeping things simple put two dots of red opposite each other and 2 dots of white opposite each other, starting on the outside of one of the dots, swirl the colours into each other in a spiral motion, ending up in the middle. Don't forget about the leaves, add a simple leaf shape in green, then using your toothpick again add a small dot of white or yellow to the base of the leaf

and pull this second colour up through the centre to the tip of the leaf.

You can make many of these stickers at the one time! Cure once you are happy with your designs, the next step is to cover your design in your gel polish clear topcoat, don't worry about overlapping your designs. Cure again for the time advised by the gel polish and wipe the dispersion layer, you can now remove, with small scissors you can trim around your design. They can be stored in small pots, it's

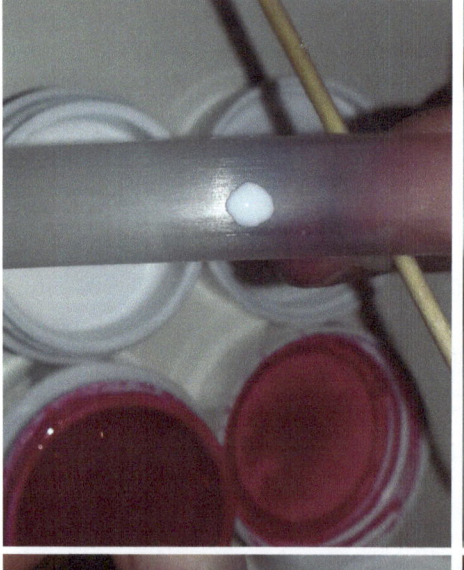
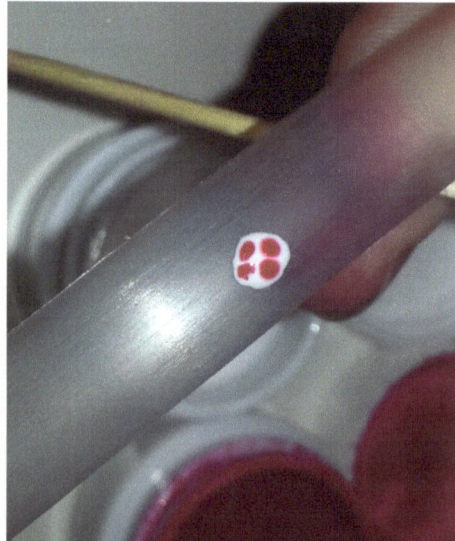
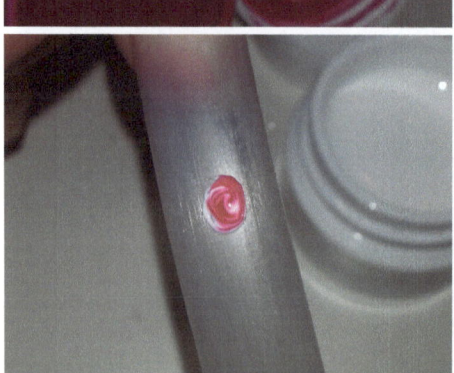
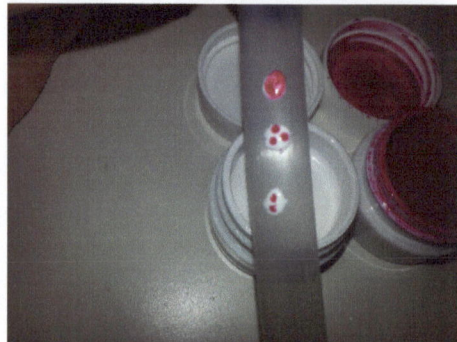

handy to apply one with nail glue to the top so you can see what stickers are inside. You can now apply your bespoke and handmade stickers sealing them in with a topcoat. Having them on pop stick or a nail art board to display is a good idea, you clients can pick what design they want.

With endless options, it can only put a smile on your clients faces, and in turn, we as therapist will be wearing a smile as well!

BEAUTY EDIT

The last weeks for me have been absolutely crazy, a makeup artists job is never the same in any one day and it's always interesting, especially the people you meet along the way. I have been busy teaching my new cohort of student's techniques in historic makeup dating back to the 1920's which are fun and interesting! one of my very talented students entered the 'Professional Beauty Competition' in Manchester and after only 6 weeks of training she managed to win second place in the 1920's category which was amazing for her and it also made me very proud. I have been busy also in between teaching, planning for many fashion shows and just recently I have been working as the head creative make-up artist for the 'Miss World' TV commercial, profiling days and the big event at London's Excel, look out for a special feature in the next Lash Inc Journal. Please read my top picks for this issue.....

Buy British is a motto I like to try and stick to where ever possible and now 'Buy Organic' is becoming a second motto I like to stick to when buying skincare. The Potion Shop and Bee Good are both environmentally friendly and it helps to reduce the carbon footprint, this issue I have trialed two British Organic skin care products and I found both of them kind and gentle on my skin, I have also noticed my skin has a brighter complexion than normal and has felt really supple with both products.

PERRON RIGOT - BROW SCULPTOR EYEBROW KIT

This highly versatile professional and retail brow defining kit is ideal for use in the salon or for maintaining brows at home between waxes. It contains four long-wearing, easily bendable sheer brow shades to suit all colourings, three stencil designs to ensure a brow contour to suit your face shape and your mood, Brow System Gel to tame and set a double-sided applicator brush and a Double Brow Pen with brow wax and highlighter. I used this product for the first time and fell in love, the box contains everything that you need to be able to achieve a high definition brow and it contains a range of colours that suit different skin tones and ages. I like the fact that you have everything you need in one box, so for makeup artists it's a great kit essential that you can carry in your kit in the knowledge that you will have all the required shades. I also had a little play with it to create an 'Ombre Brow' which turned out beautiful; the product is easy to use and long lasting, a kit that I would highly recommend.

10/10

020 7512 0872

/enquiry@thalgo.co.uk @PerronRigotUK

http://www.perron-rigot.co.uk/en/catalogue/produit/brow-system-sculptor-kit.8-613.html

---

BEE GOOD

The philosophy of the Bee Good range is centuries old, they use British Honey, propolis and beeswax in their range of products that come from sustainable sources and none of their products contain any synthetic colours, mineral oil, silicones or parabens, which are all bad for us. We should be reading the labels of our skincare to try and avoid using any of the aforementioned ingredients as they have all been clinically proven to damage the skin. They never test on animals and the bees are not harmed at all through the process of making the products.

Our all natural cream cleanser is suitable for all skin types.

This Honey & Propolis 2 in 1 cream cleanser sweeps away make-up and grime without drying out your skin. Used with the included pure muslin cloth to gently exfoliate, it leaves skin bee-autifully clean, soft and silky-smooth. The benefits of this Bee Good cream cleanser include British propolis which possesses well known 'healing' and 'antimicrobial' properties, and has been used for centuries for medicinal and healthcare purposes. The 2 in 1 cleanser also has anti-bacterial properties making it one of the best ingredients for balancing problematic skins.

I used the product morning and night; I massaged a small amount onto dry skin, over the face and neck. Wet the cloth in warm water, wring out and gently wipe away the debris and makeup away with the soft cloth, I repeated the process to ensure my skin was deeply cleaned, I loved the product and found it extra nourishing especially in these cold winter months.

http://beegood.co.uk/

@BeeGood_UK

POTIONSHOP

The Potionshop cleansing gel number 1 is organic and paraben free, ideal for facial cleansing everyday to remove even the heaviest of makeups.

This product left my skin feeling soft and supple and smelling really good. I loved the fact that I could massage the product into my skin get in a hot shower and the makeup from the day would just melt away without even a trace of mascara, I then got out the shower and did a second cleanse just to cleanse deep down and to remove all traces of excess oil as my skin can get pretty oily during the day. Apply to the skin – take a pea size portion of the gel on a fingertip and massage into the face, rinse with warm water, the gel will then turn to a milky consistency. Rinse well with warm water and blot skin dry. This Potionshop Cleansing gel will leave your skin refreshed and hydrated – it contains NO detergent so will not strip your skin of its natural oils. Clients with the most sensitive of skin love this product. I loved the smell of Rose in this product and that it is PH 6.5 and all of the products are not tested on animals.

@potionshop
http://www.potionshop.co.uk/

ORGANIC LASH SERUM

My last product this month is the Ogenic Lash serum that promises to help your lashes grow thicker and longer. I have been trialing this product for two months now and I am absolutely over the moon with it, everyone has commented on my lashes and how fabulous they look, even being mistaken for false lashes on a couple of occasions. This is my favourite product of the month and I love that it actually works! 10/10

A little more detail about the product....

Eyelashes have an extremely short growth cycle coupled with a much longer resting period. This is the opposite of normal hair growth and means that over 90% of a human eyelash is in the 'resting' period at any one time.

The key to increased eyelash length is to break the cycle: reducing the resting period and increasing the period of the growth phase.

In tests, OGENIC® Eyelash growth serum is proven to increase the length and thickness of eyelashes. Get longer, beautiful looking lashes in 60 days.

90% of women in a clinical study showed an overall improvement in their eyelashes.

OGENIC® repairs hair fibres that are thin, undernourished or weakened whilst helping to protect healthy lashes from further damage. All ingredients are non-irritating and comply with EU safety regulations.

- An effective combination of potent polypeptides, vitamins, minerals and natural botanicals.
- Helps minimise breakage.
- Help lashes to recover from environmental, chemical and physical damage.
- Proven to naturally improve the length (3mm – 9mm extra) and thickness of eyelashes.
- Exclusive Amino10 Protein ComplexTM supports the natural renewal cycle of eyelashes.
- Vitamins, botanicals and conditioners fortify, help protect and revitalise the eyelashes.
- Prostaglandin free.
- Ophthalmologist safety tested; clinically and dermatologist tested.
- Fragrance, colourant and paraben free.
- At least 2-3 months supply in each 6ml bottle.

COLLEGE TRAINING VERSUS PRIVATE TRAINING

If you are considering a career in the Beauty industry there are a few issues you may want to consider beforehand to establish which route you should take and which will work best for you.

If you are already a qualified beauty/holistic therapist, lash technician or nail technician you may be considering additional training to enhance your portfolio, this article will help you decide which route to take.

We all have different lifestyles and commitments, so what works for one person may not suit you, take into consideration some of the points listed below.

COLLEGE PROS

• More hours spent in class with supervision from trainer, if you are practising at home you won't have the trainer there to keep you right. You may find it difficult to commit to practice outwith college hours.

• New friends and relationships can be formed when you are attending college for a period of time. It gives you a chance to socialise with people who are interested in the same industry as yourself.

• More funding is available through government schemes in colleges compared to private training providers. This can make a huge difference to some people.

• More time for practical work as you will be attending regularly and carrying out practical work on a constant basis with supervision from

trainer.
- Childcare facilities are available for people undertaking full time college courses.
- External or additional courses are sometimes available to advance or further your education.

PRIVATE PROS
- Qualifications are obtained in a short period of time as private courses are usually from 1 day to 5 days training depending on the qualification.
- Private training providers tend to have smaller groups which may suit some people who don't feel comfortable in larger groups and may feel overwhelmed. In a smaller group some people may find it easier to ask questions and speak out if there is anything they are not sure of during the training period.
- Smaller groups can mean more one to one time with the trainer, they will have more time to spend individually with students compared to training a large number of people.
- Private training providers tend to keep more up to date with new trends and training and can be more versatile with courses they offer.
- Private training providers are more flexible in the courses they offer which means students can build up their portfolio and only undertake courses they are interested in learning.

COLLEGE CONS
- It takes longer to qualify as most courses are offered on a full time/ part time or evening timetable.
- College groups tend to be much larger, some people may find this intimidating and would prefer a smaller intimate environment.
- College lecturers may have less time to spend with individual students due to large numbers in classes and timetables can be strict, they may not have time for questions or problems after class.
- More time will be spent in class covering theory work which some people would prefer to do at home after initial practical training.
- You have to commit to the college timetable once you have enrolled on your course and attend regularly to avoid missing any tuition within the course so as not to fall behind.

PRIVATE CONS
- As most private training courses are short and fast track you may not have time to get to know your fellow students or build new friendships.
- Private training can be expensive with less funding available compared to college training.
- Most private courses will be self funded.
- You will have a limited period of time to spend on practical work so you have to commit to lots of practice outwith the training course.
- Finding reputable training schools can be quite difficult as there are many offering training which may not be accredited by an awarding body or charging huge training fees for not much training.

I have 5 years of experience working as a college lecturer and 4 years of experience as a private trainer, both have been very rewarding and I have met some lovely people during my teaching career. In my opinion it depends on each individual which route they should take, if you are opting for college training it is a very big commitment as far as attendance is concerned, whereas with private training you will spend much less time attending but will have to commit to working hard out with the training days.

Whatever route you decide to go, do your research and find out as much information as you can before making a commitment.

Working in the beauty industry is hard work but a very rewarding career, be prepared to set aside sufficient time for studying and practicing. Keep up to date with new trends and aim to be the best you possibly can. There is huge competition in regards to our industry and I'm sure this will continue in the future so it is worth considering all the facts before you commit to any training.

Below are quotes from Ellen Stewart and Carolyn Carroll. Ellen is currently a college lecturer within the Beauty Therapy department of New College Lanarkshire, she has experienced both college and private training, as has Carolyn, who owns The Beauty Post Salon for Beauty and Holistic treatments.

Here are their thoughts on college versus private:

Ellen Stewart, Beauty Therapy Lecturer, New College Lanarkshire.

"I think college training offers inclusion in that, it's accessible to everyone regardless of ability, financial status and, personal restrictions, like child care. College courses however, tend to have large numbers in each class and the curriculum is set within strict guidelines with limited resources determined by tight budgets. Private training can be expensive, therefore not always accessible, but offers training in smaller numbers, so more one to one attention, and courses are on line with current up to date trends."

Carolyn Carroll, owner of The Beauty Post.

"I found with following private training that I had more confidence in my treatments due to more personalised instruction from my trainer. Any areas that I struggled with were picked up quicker than in a college environment due to large class numbers. I feel I have more confidence and skills carrying out nail treatments than the students that studied in college, and they have agreed with me."

I hope this helps in some small way to guide you on the correct career choice for you!

Kim Gibb
kim.gibb@blueyonder.co.uk

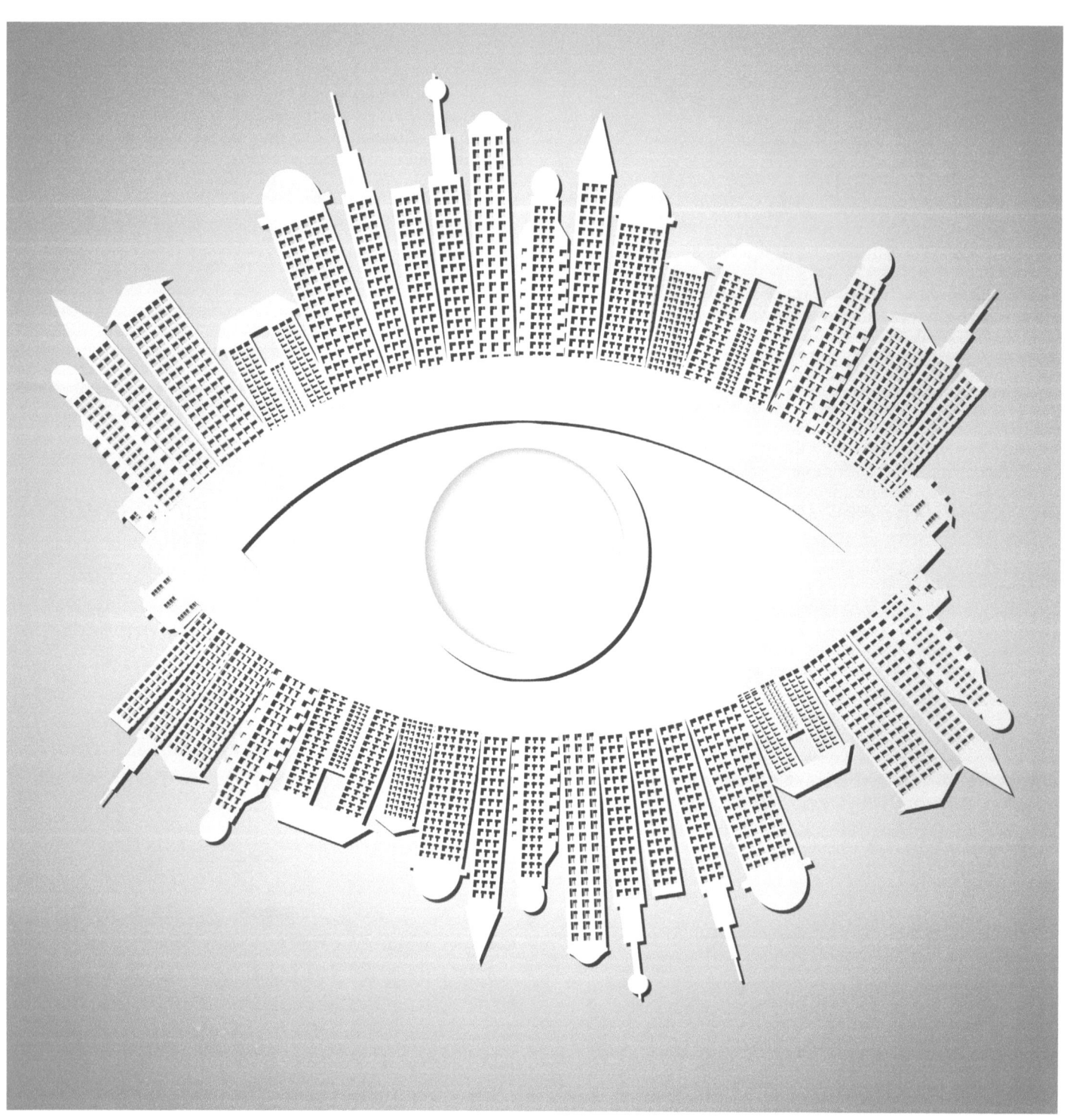

Business

The results are in for **Best Eyelash Supplier**.
We had 2 categories Europe and USA & Canada.

Congratulations to
SugarLash (Best Eyelash Supplier – USA & Canada) *voted by eyelash technicians via the Lash Artist of the Year – Facebook group.*

http://www.sugarlashpro.com/

How does it feel to have won multiple awards and be recognised by other lash artists?

A. It is so great to win this award as a fairly new company to emerge in North America for supplies! I am thrilled that lash artists are loving our products and finding that we are an asset to their business. It validates all the sleepless nights, and endless hours of research, testing, experimenting, and work that went into creating our brand of supplies. My husband thought I was crazy to start a supply company with so much on the go -- but now he works (more) than full time as the head of our shipping department! We are so blessed to be on this adventure together, and we are so thankful to all of our Sugarlash customers globally!

Why do you think you were voted the best eyelash supplier for USA & Canada.

A. I think Sugarlash's performance speaks for itself. We have some of the most luxurious lash supplies in the world, and we get constant feedback from lash artists that tell us that their clients are noticing a difference in how their lashes, look, feel, and retain. Some of our most popular products are:

-Our two best selling adhesives: Candylash,

and Elite which are very thin, instant grab, low to no fumes, and last up to 8 weeks.

-Our lash extension lines: Soho Silk lashes, and Uptown (faux) Mink. Both are beautifully tapered, double treated for amazing curl retention, and finished in a rich jet back (no blue) hue. Our lashes come in: B, C, D, L, and L+ curls // Lengths 5mm-16mm // and diamaters 0.05, 0.06, 0.07, 0.10, 0.12, 0.15, and 0.18!

-Our speciality lash trays which include: Bottom Lash Trays (5mm-8mm) in a universal "soft b" curl that suits any eye/lash type for lower lash application, our "Greater Lengths" Tray which is a mix of 14-16mm for those clients who can handle more length than our traditional mixed lash trays offer (7mm-13mm), and our *coming soon* Eyelight colour lash palettes!

-Our precision tweezers and tools have had rave reviews and aren't even out yet!

As a company, we are focused on top performance of our lash products, as well as an awesome price, and supporting our customers to keep their profit margins high. We only work with manufacturers who are willing to develop new items for us and tweak the formulations and processes to be authentic, one of a kind Sugarlash products. This is why you won't find our quality elsewhere - it is 100% unique to our brand, and has been tested, tweaked, and perfected to meet my high standards for look and performance. We want to be our customers one-stop shop so they can save themselves from high shipping charges which cut from their bottom profit margin. With this in mind, we have minimum order requirements for FREE shipping (worldwide). More than half of our customers order ALL lash needs from us and literally pay $0/ year for shipping -- How amazing is that?!

What sets Sugarlash apart from other suppliers?

A. I think Sugarlash is loved so much because we understand the needs and desires of customers, lash artists, and business owners. I have been on all sides of the industry. I have been a consumer (before I got into doing lashes) so I knew what I looked for, and wanted in a lash line -- including aftercare, marketing, and brand representation. I also am a lash artist and learned what kind of lash extensions

I like as far as taper, flex, colour etc. I learned what kind of adhesive worked best for myself as a technician and for my clientele to get long lasting results-- and I learned what type of products were essentials vs non-essentials in a lash business. I have then been an owner of a large scale lash lounge and quickly learned how much ordering large quantities from multiple companies costs a business with shipping and import duties -- I learned that there was a need in the market for a lash supplier to carry EVERYTHING a successful lash business needed, and how crucial it is to offer free shipping order minimums to keep profits high for lash artists. Now, as a trainer and supplier my priorities are to provide lash artists with every top-performing product they will need for their lash business, and to do it in a high-end luxury look and feel that attracts them the right kind of clientele. I am thoroughly enjoying building relationships with our customers around the world and custom-creating new products for them based on feedback they give us and requests they make for their market.

I truly take great pride in supporting the business success of others. After having so much success in the industry as a lash artist, and salon owner -- I want others to experience those rewards in their own business. It is truly humbling to know that all the success

Sugarlash has, is because we are aiding in the success so many customers around the world! We have customers in 30 countries around the world, and I couldn't be more inspired to keep the lash industry (and their businesses) evolving, progressing, and thriving.

What does the future have in store for you?

A. Sugarlash is getting a facelift as we speak! Sugarlash over the next few months is getting a website, and packaging overhaul. We are also getting new supplies including:

-Our own brand of LashLift kits and supplies

-A lash extension aftercare line including cleanser, sealant, mascara, growth serum, eyeliners, precision lash combs, and sleep masks.

-An aftercare line for our eyebrow extension supplies which includes: Brow liners, cleanser, and brushes.

-Our new Eyelight Colour lash line which will have specially designed colour palettes to make certain eye colours "pop", as well as single colour trays in both subtle and bold hues.

-Our swiss-made LashPRO Precision line of tweezers, designed by myself for perfect angles, closures, and performance.

We also have launched our pilot Brand Ambassador program for Sugarlash enthusiasts with perks such as: Getting to trial and test new products and prototypes, buying opportunities before public launches of new product, having a crucial role in the development of new products, and more!

Thank you so much again for the honour of this award!! We can't wait to bring the industry more breakthrough products in 2015!

With Love
Loreta L.

expect from any other Lash supplier. We only try to fulfil our customers needs.

What sets Flawless Lashes apart from other suppliers?

A. Flawless Lashes continuously strives to source THE most up-to-date, luxurious products on the market today at an affordable price. Loretta's drive and passion for perfection is evident in the products she showcases. She personally stays in touch with her customers, through an online forum, emails, communicating with them as to when she is running special offers, or might be out of stock of something for a short while, etc. etc. Deliveries are extremely prompt and free gifts are often added to packages, making customers feel very special indeed!

What does the future have in store for you?

A. There are plenty of new plans, ideas, we wont stop searching for better! This coming new year we already have something very excited to be added in stock, some events etc.

*Congratulations to **Flawless Lashes** on being voted as (**Best Eyelash Supplier – Europe**) by lash technicians via the Lash Artist of the Year – Facebook group.*

http://flawlesslashesproducts.co.uk/

How does it feel to have won multiple awards and be recognised by other lash artists?

A. I Feel honoured , cant describe how amazing it feels, hard work really pays off . Love this industry .

Why do you think you were voted the best eyelash supplier for Europe?

A. First of all I would like to say a huge Thank you , for those who voted, we promise that our service will get better and better.

Why we were voted as a best supplier in Europe? I guess this question could be answered by our customers. We don't do anything special, nothing that you wouldn't

FLAWLESS L'LASHES
Loretta's Lash Academy & Beautique

BULIDING YOUR BUSINESS

Francine Widdows

The things we have to do to build our business and the prices we should charge our clients.

Having decided to finally put my prices up and start charging more for my time, I was disappointed when three of my regular clients decided they didn't want lash extensions any more - coincidence or not?

I was pondering over these clients, trying to understand whether it was something I had done, or if they were unhappy with my service etc. Then when I thought a little more and came to realise that these were clients that I had been very lenient with - allowed to reschedule appointments at last minute, arrive with make up on and not get tough with them, or come back with fewer lashes than 50% (more like four on each eye) and I always topped up for an infill price despite it being nearly a full set. Taking this into consideration I believed that these clients may have realised that now they won't be getting their full sets for infill prices and that's the last I will see of them. But then who's fault was it, theirs for not maintaining their lashes, or me for not setting my rules and being strict from the start?

However, I'm very good at looking at things from a different perspective and I then began to consider the following.
When I was building my business I didn't have the good client base that I have now, instead I was grateful for any client that booked in and then re booked with me. I had to chase clients, give them a little bit extra, be lenient when they didn't look after their lashes and returned with just a few hanging on.

I did at the time what I had to do to build my business, to keep clients happy and to earn a living. By doing what I did and accommodating clients like this I gradually built my client base and over time had more than enough clients to ensure I was fully booked week after week. It's better to have had the clients in and allowed

them to bend the rules a little, if I had been strict from the start then I may have alienated them and have been left with just a few.

However now that I am very busy I do not have the time to accommodate clients like this and I can afford to lose clients that will not follow their aftercare, look after their lashes, keep their appointments and lastly respect my business. So if you are still building your business and you are feeling frustrated with clients like this, just remember that you will not always have to accommodate them. Look at these clients as people that you provide a great service to and use them to practice your skills on. Then as your business gets busier and busier you can set more strict rules, keeping those clients that abide by them and losing the ones that do not.

Moving on from this it's also important to understand how much to charge your clients. When you first enter the industry of Eyelash Extensions you must charge in accordance to your standard of work. A new technician is not going to be producing amazing work so bear this in mind with your prices. Charge lower prices to start off with, this will attract lots of clients wanting "cheaper lashes". It's unlikely that these clients will be good regulars but they will give you all the practice you need. Then over time gradually increase your prices as your standard of lashing improves. Aim to put your prices up once or twice a year with April and the end of November being good times as they head into the busy lash season.
Don't forget to look at the average price of lashes in the area that you live in, as this will help to dictate what you charge. Also remember to charge for the standard of work you are producing as a result of the time, effort and financial investment you have made into any additional training, as well as looking at the standard of work of your local competition. Taking all of that into consideration you must also be realistic - since putting my prices up(

in the last 6 weeks) I have had a big decrease in the amount of new enquiries and booking I usually receive - because I'm now quite expensive for the area that I live in. I feel that I should be charging a lot more than my current prices because I am the only lash specialist in my area, I constantly take additional training and I produce good work in comparison to my very poor local competition. However my town is saturated with students and an older population, neither of the two want or have the disposable income for lash extensions. So you can see how important it is to adjust your prices to your standard of work and your location.

The most important thing to remember is that this is your business and you can take all the advice given, but ultimately it's your decision to run your business how you see fit and charge what you are worth. Building your business is a journey and you must learn from it and tweak it as and when you need be. As long as you provide an excellent service to your clients and continue to learn you will succeed.

LASH MEET UPS
Social night out or educational opportunity?

So what is a lash meet up? A lash meet up is a group of lashers who meet up to 'talk shop'. If organised correctly it can be a great educational experience. You could can have guest speakers, competitions and an open forum question and answer session.

Training providers are ideally suited to run these events, as they are likely to have more space than a therapist and also have a good contact list of people to invite.

The social side: It can be a great opportunity to chill out, get away from work and home and be with like minded people.

I recently attended Sinful Lashes first lash meet up in Los Angeles. As well as being an educational event it was fun, with prizes, great food and bubbly. After this event I decided that Lash Inc would like to support people organising events of this type.

If you would like to organise your own event in your country, (any country or city) then please email me for details on support we can give.

Here are a few photos of the Los Angeles meet up. I hope to see photos of your meet ups soon.

Louise Prunty
info@lashinc.eu

ASK FOR REFERRALS

An easy way to get more clients

Ask for them - sound too easy?

So you have some really happy clients you can confidently ask them to recommend them to their friends. Doing it verbally is ok, but you want to be able to reward them and also find out who your best referrers are. Try to reward the referrer and new customer in some way.

Get Referrals example 1:
On your consultation form at the end have...

_____

Please list your friends who you think would like to try my service. They will get $x off the service and you will get $x off your next appointment.

Name..

Number or Email ....

_____

Have space for 4 names and numbers, on average you will get 3 names and numbers, so 3 new leads and on average 1 new booking.

Example 2:
Give client referral cards that they can give to their friends or even business cards, have a tracking code or the referrer name on it.

Example 3:
Set clients / customers up with a link that has a unique tracking code. Then you can track who is sending you referrals and reward them.

Can you think of a few other ways you could generate referrals?

CPD QUESTIONS

FOR CONTINUAL PROFESSIONAL DEVELOPMENT

**Email your answers to
sarah@lashinc.eu
to gain your CPD certificate.**

1) How do you deal with "hooded" eyelids?

2) Name 2 different ways to prime lashes.

3) Explain how volume lashes differ to classic lash extensions.

4) In a volume set of eyelash extensions how many eyelashes are usually used?

5) Name 2 advantages of private lash education over public college.

6) Name 2 things you have learned from our 'Building Your Business' article.

7) Name a method to use in asking for referrals.

8) After reading Patch testing in the UK, what is your opinion or conclusion?

9) Why is it so important to aim for a moisture free environment for applying lashes?

WELCOME TO OUR WEBINAR

INTRODUCING LASH INC AMBASSADORS & LASH INC WEBINARS

Lash Inc Ambassadors:

Are you an educator / trainer? Passionate about education and the industry?
We are looking for Lash Inc Ambassadors to share what Lash Inc has to offer as an educational tool.
Each ambassador will get a package of free products and services for their training school and their students.
Interested? Please email info@lashinc.eu

Lash Inc Webinars:

We have produced our first webinar featuring...

1) Chrissanthie Cosmetics
2) My Brand Lashes
3) Flawless Lashes

Great educational content, this particular webinar is free to Lash Inc subscribers.

You can access it at ...
http://youtu.be/Wf_XwNpaIqs

Join our Lash Inc Magazine Facebook group to be informed of future Webinars.

Lash Inc
Accreditation

United Kingdom & Ireland
Accredited Training Providers.

ENGLAND:

Love My Lashes
Sue Winter
7 Bremen Grove, Shenley Brook End,
Milton Keynes
MK5 7FJ
mklashes@gmail.com

Flirties
Unit 2, Tarlair Business Park
Tarlair Way,
Macduff
AB44 1RU
www.flirties.co.uk
0845 022 22 33

East Anglian Beauty Training
maureen@eabt.co.uk
www.eabt.co.uk

Sugarlash Academy of Lash Artistry
Vicky Rugg
www.sugarlashpro.com
info@sweetsugarlashes.com

SCOTLAND:

Caledonian Therapy Academy
7 Newton Place
Glasgow
G3 7PR
www.ctacademy.co.uk
Tel: 01423329251

Flirties
Unit 2, Tarlair Business Park
Tarlair Way,
Macduff
AB44 1RU
www.flirties.co.uk
0845 022 22 33

United States Of America
Accredited Training Providers.

Benita Lash Studio
18321 W. Lake Houston Pkwy
Suite 305
Humble,
TX 77346
benitaramos@outlook.com

Australia & New Zealand
Accredited Training Providers.

Komao
Kerrie Ann Ditz

Sugarlash Academy of Lash Artistry
Melena Langford
www.sugarlashpro.com
info@sweetsugarlashes.com

South Africa
Accredited Training Providers.

Luscious Lashes International
Lesley Altree
6 Hutchinson Ave, Table View, 7441
South Africa
Lesleyann@iafrica.com

Adele Sutton Training
72 Steve Biko str
Jubilee Square
Potchefstroom
North West
South Africa
www.adelesutton.com
info@adelesutton.com
+27 763119011

Canada
Accredited Training Providers.

Sugarlash Academy
of Lash Artistry
Courtney Buhler
www.sugarlashpro.com
info@sweetsugarlashes.com
587.982.5274

Worldwide
Accredited Training Providers.

Deluxe Lashes International
Aleksandra Maniuse
+37060922922
info@deluxelashes.lt
www.deluxelashes.lt
www.deluxe-lashes.com

SUPPLIER DIRECTORY

USA & Canada

SkynLash Academy
Training Courses
Continuing Education at it's Finest

Skype Training Available
Basic Lashes to Advanced Volume
Lashcoat & Lashbrow Training
SkynLash Shop for the Finest Lash
Supplies
www.skinlashstudio.com
info@skinlashstudio.com
732-618-2096 NJ USA

Aesthetic Image is the professional's source for innovative and luxury lash products. We offer the highest quality lashes, adhesives, and cutting edge lash tools. Our exclusive Pro Lash System provides lash artists with a faster and more efficient way to lash. We ship worldwide. Shop 24/7 online at ailashes.com
info@ailashes.com / ailashes.com

Sugar Lash
Eyelash extension & training provider

www.sweetsugarlashes.com
www.facebook.com/sugarlashPRO

Lash Affair by J.Paris
www.LashAffair.com
info@lashaffair.com
1.800.608.2420
We sell Luxury Lash Extension Products & Global Certifications
We ship and train globally as well.

United Kingdom

Flirties
BeautyTrix
Tel. 0845 022 2233
www.beautytrix.me

Lash Perfect
0208 500 9028
info@lashperfect.co.uk
www.lashperfect.co.uk

- Professional and accredited training available from expert trainers at competitive prices throughout the UK
- Internationally renowned and available worldwide through over 25 overseas distributors

Nouveau Lash
Nouveau Beauty Group
http://www.nouveaubeautygroup.com/

Tel: 0844 8016820

Novalash
http://www.novalash.com/
contact@novalash.com
1-866-430-1261

RevitaLash® Cosmetics
cservice@revitalash.com
www.revitalash.com

Sweet Lash
www.sweetlash.com
info@sweetlash.com
377 Marshall Way N #1
Layton, UT 84041

My Beautiful Eyes
Mylash, Myscara, Mybrows
http://www.mybeautifuleyes.eu/
sales@beautyinnovator.co.uk

United Kingdom

NOVALASH®
EYELASH EXTENSIONS

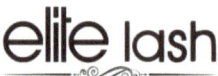

UK / Europe

Novalash
http://www.novalash.com/uk/
CONTACT@NOVALASH.COM
+44(0)1273 862399

elite lash

UK/Ireland

http://www.elitelash.co.uk/
Elite Lash Academy
Mall Road
Monaghan
Ireland
Tel: +3534772580
+353868593699
Email: santa.jodka@gmail.com

Denmark / Europe

LASH COMPANY

www.lashcompany.dk
Webshop: www.shop.lashcompany.dk
LASH COMPANY, Beringsvej 7,
7500 Holstebro Denmark
Email: info@lashcompany.dk
Supply Denmark & Worldwide

South Africa

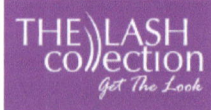

THE LASH collection
Get The Look

The Lash Collection

http://www.thelashcollection.co.za/
info@thelashcollection.co.za

LUSCIOUS LASHES
EYELASH EXTENSIONS

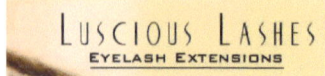

Luscious Lashes International

http://www.eyelashextensions.co.za/
Email: lushlashes@iafrica.com
+27 (0) 72 338 7000

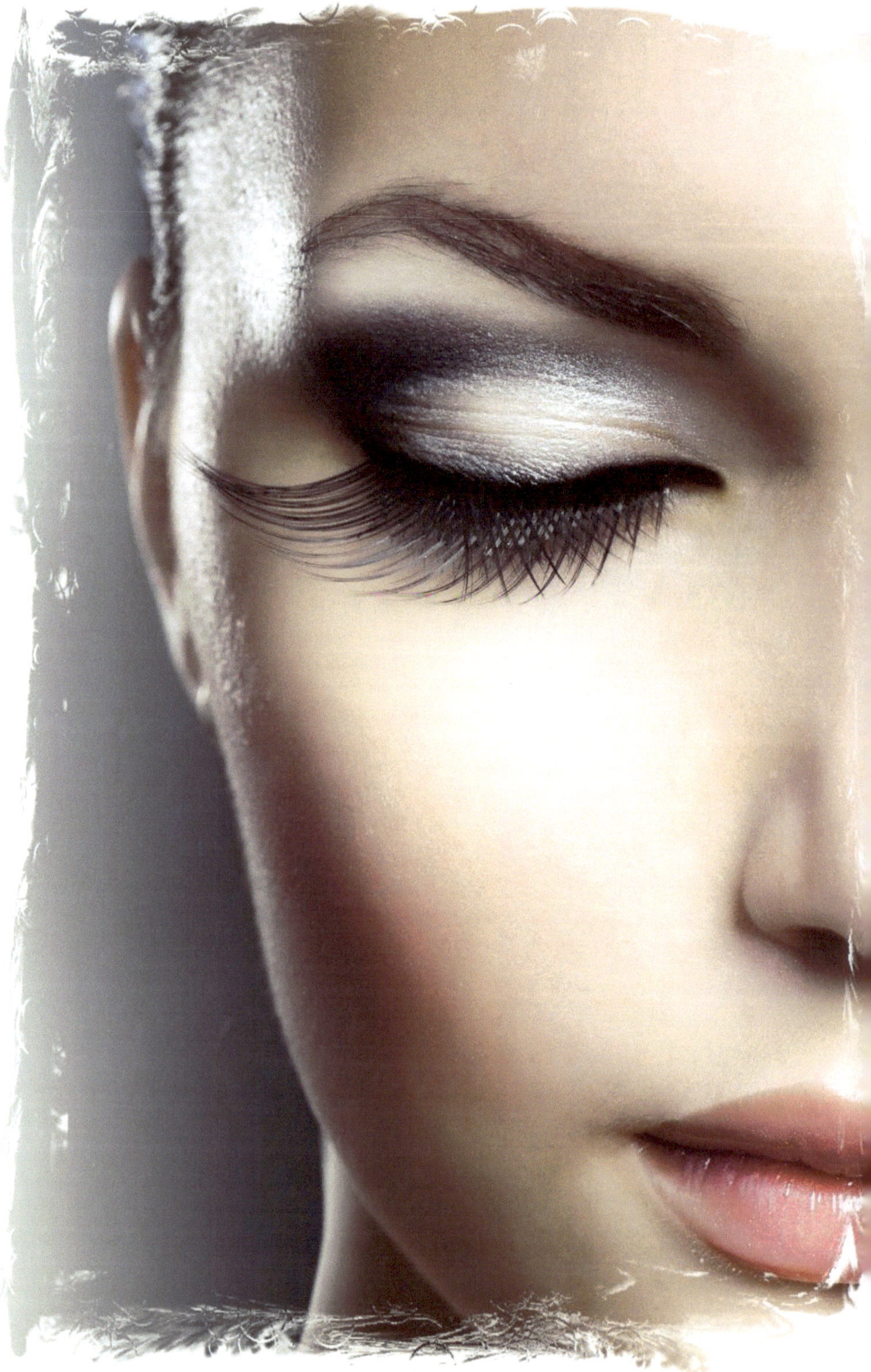

VZ Hair and Glamour Ltd

International Distributor - Affordable Beauty Supplies
T: +44 (0)755 492 5551
E: info@vzhairandglamour.com
W: www.vzhairandglamour.com

• Professional LashBlack 3 Week Semi Permanent Mascara: Made in England & EU Certified
• Eyelash Extension Medical Grade Glues made in England – Ultra Diamond Pro:
fast drying - Senses for Sensitive eyes: low vapour odour, perfect for trainers and beginners
• Individual Mink Eyelashes 100% Real Siberian Handmade Lashes